To Russia With Love
The Children's Stories

Debbie Deegan
with Emily Hourican

Principal Photography
Larisa Ershova

With contributions from
Brendan O'Connor
Damien O'Connor
Mary Kennedy
Joanna Fortune
Patricia McGrath
Egor Zubets

All royalties from the sale of this book go directly to
To Russia With Love.
We thank you for your support.

TO RUSSIA WITH L♥VE

Text **HUG** to **50300** to donate €4 to our Charity.
100% of text cost goes to To Russia With Love across most network providers.
Some providers apply VAT which means a minimum of €3.26 will go to To Russia With Love.
Service Provider LIKECHARITY 014433890

To Russia With Love
The Children's Stories

First published 2014

This edition published 2014 © Debbie Deegan and Emily Hourican

The moral right of the author(s) has been asserted.

A catalogue record for this book is available from the British Library.

ISBN: 978-0-9548653-9-9

Printing

GraficasCems, Spain

Papers used in the printing of this book are natural, recyclable products made from wood grown in sustainable forests; the manufacturing processes conform to the environmental regulations of the country of origin.

I would like to dedicate this book to the beautiful, brave children that
we work with every day.
They have brought so much more to our lives,
than we can ever bring to theirs.

Debbie Deegan, October 2014.

Dea Rob and Kristina,

I hope you like the book,
it is a tapestry of love
energy, passion, wove with
Irish and Russian hands,

Debbie

Introduction
Brendan O'Connor

Editor of the Sunday Independent Life Magazine and host of RTE's The Saturday Night Show, Brendan has known Debbie for 15 years, and has acted as compere and host for To Russia With Love events, and at awards during which Debbie has been honoured.

Her heart bursts. It bursts so much sometimes it spills out all over you. Or down the phone. It bursts with sad stories and tiny heartbreaking details, all the hurt she sees and carries around inside her. And sometimes she just seems to need to spill some of it out, to tell someone. So you'll randomly get a string of the longest texts. Maybe someone hasn't come through and has decided to end it all, the worst kind of negation of the work she does. Or it could be just an image: how they sit at the window looking out at Christmas waiting for their parents to come.

I don't remember when I first met Debbie. But instantly she treats you like she knows you. She has that great gift of familiarity. Which is only a gift when it's welcomed I guess, but with her it is welcome. Her instant connection is presumably what made her see these faraway children as her own too. She took them on because she didn't see why you wouldn't. They were children. Faraway ones. Strangers. But she just treated them like she knew them. What else would she do?

Brendan O'Connor and Debbie Deegan: "She never lets us forget. She never lets anyone forget."

So then she does her next trick, which is to draw you in. Whenever she saw what it was she saw that sucked her in, those kids found the best saleswoman they could ever get. She doesn't so much encourage you to buy the cause, she envelops you into it. It's a hug crossed with a death grip. And then you are in.

And she never lets us forget. She never lets anyone forget. Because she knows it is easy to forget. She knows that the more we had our own problems here, the easier it became to forget. But she couldn't forget it so she couldn't let us forget it. It torments her in the dark hours and it drives her in her waking hours. And she catches us all up in her whirlwind. And when we flag, she senses it and she reminds you of the children again.

Behind the whirlwind is a strange patience too. While the system and the Russians frustrate her she plays ball with them too. And she flirts and charms and barracks her way through them as well. How she deals with the Russians is always a mystery. It is not something she burdens our suburban minds with. We understand at some level that she had to go native, to become one of them in order to truly understand them. But she knows we don't need to know that. She deals with the ambivalences and the ambiguities there so she can keep it simple and heartfelt for us.

The strange patience is such that she waited years for me to fully understand. She just kept me there and waited and waited. She knew I would have a child myself, eventually, and that then and only then would I understand. And I did. And then she said, "Now you really get it".

But she is not a saint. She is a force of nature and a force of fierce morality but she is worldly with it. She knows that rivers of tears are not enough. She knows you have to do the politics as well. She knows you have to get people drunk and show them a good time. She knows you have to have the bestest parties, and that you have be the bestest performer at those parties. She knows that we are all only human beings with egos at the end of the day and that, unlike her, we can easily forget. And then she reminds you. Because she can never forget whatever it is she sees every time she looks in their eyes.

✳

Playtime in Hortolova: "They were children. Faraway ones. Strangers. But she just treated them like she knew them. What else would she do?"

Prologue
Debbie Deegan

Dubliner Debbie Deegan is a married mother of three and has dedicated the last 17 years to running the Irish charity 'To Russia with Love'. She has received many awards for her work with the charity, including the Rehab International Person of the Year (2009); UNESCO Tolerance Award Winner (2010) as well as numerous citations from Russia. She holds diplomas in child psychology and childcare and has spoken around the world about her experiences.

When Emily and I started writing this second book, I was in a strange place in my head. I have spent 16 years fighting children's battles, constantly questioning what is right and if we are doing the best thing. Now, I am being forced to think in a different way about what we do, and I have some issues with that.

The EU tells us daily that we should not be supporting children's homes, not be strengthening orphanages, not using all our energies behind the walls of these institutions, but trying to get the children out, out to foster care, out to families, out to anywhere that is not an institution.

After many years of learning on the job and from our own mistakes, To Russia With Love and the EU experts know the way forward, we have seen the mistakes made. We know the way we should be strengthening society. Good people like our own MEP

Debbie holding an infant during one of her many trips to Hortolova

Mairead McGuinness are bringing about much positive change in that area. However the world behind our orphanage walls still exists and will continue to exist for many years to come. Russia is committed to moving away from the orphanage system but this will inevitably take time. The children in the orphanages need to be helped now. Not just with physical needs but with a secure and loving emotional environment. This is our mission. To help these children overcome often traumatic pasts and to achieve their dreams.

I am sitting typing this on a flight to Moscow. Once again, orphanage life spreads out before me – endless problems, institutionalized staff, broken-hearted children, cold rooms, low budgets, worn old books, threadbare shoes, a meagre, loveless existence, our smiling children waiting for us to arrive. Some of our older children are leaving this week; many of them have nowhere to go and no one to care what becomes of them.

Unfortunately two world wars, a civil war, a revolution and internal political and economic strife created many orphans, and Russia has only in the last decade or so been in a position to begin to address the legacy of orphanages that this history has left it. I do not mean to criticize the Russian system but to support the efforts of the Russian government to improve, even if we are only drops in that vast ocean. I have worked with and under the skin of Russian institutions for 16 years. I know every single nuance of them. I respect their commitment to children and they respect mine.

My colleagues in Russia know how much I love their country and how much respect I have for the administrators, medical staff, teachers and carers who are seeking to bring about change. I have huge respect for the Russian system, and I hope and believe that they know I will not criticize it unless I really need to, and that if I do, it will be for the children's safety and wellbeing, and to the correct people, rather than to the tabloid press, who simply want negativity and drama. Russia-bashing is far too common in the West, so much that I am ashamed of our Western press at times. They have immense influence and it is abused way too often.

As an EU citizen, I like the idea of 'ideal' and yes, I see the damage done to vulnerable children by institutions every day. But I am a woman who works to her gut feeling, and when I know there are still thousands of little ones, unloved behind walls, often in a cold emotional environment, I for one, want to be there with these children. Beside their beds reading fairy stories, plaiting their hair, or letting them plait mine, painting their nails, tucking them in, helping them read, doing jigsaws, standing with them in court-rooms when they try and unravel their complicated pasts, shoulder to shoulder with them as they graduate with one eye always on the gate, desperately hoping a family member will come, and seeing their disappointment when nobody does. I have attended so many graduations over 16 years, and I could count on one hand the amount of times we have had visitors from the children's birth families.

We fill the gap of their missing mothers and family as best we can. That is all we can do.

Nothing else.

I have just finished reading a book on the plane, *White on Black*, by Ruben Gallego. A short, shocking, incredible story about a boy with cerebral palsy raised in one of Russia's many children's homes some years back – he went straight on to live in an old people's home at 16, because the only other option for him was an insane asylum. Reading the details of his horrendous childhood, I could see complete accuracy in his account – no drama, just pain, abandonment, shocking loneliness, and then his sheer elation when the occasional kindness was shown to him; "a fig, a mouthful of chocolate, a conversation …fed his passion to live".

He was left alone in rooms for years at a time, staring at a ceiling. On one occasion a pretty Spanish volunteer came to talk to him, "an enchanting luxury, too much for my psyche." One visit, one act of kindness, remembered forever. However, this could have been Ireland as easily as Russia – there are still patients languishing in St Ita's in Portrane and other similar places for decades with no visitors.

I knew as I closed the last page that every moment we spend doing what we do is right.

> "Institutions, whether past or current, are simply not suitable places for children. Children need their mother's love, family, hugs, kisses, encouragement."

This is us. Multiple acts of kindness? Not really. Just being human and decent to those who see very little of either.

Sometimes I think we dress up what we do too much. We are quite simple, and not wonderful humanitarians at all. We pay for visits to the dentist, for cooking lessons, sports training, art, extra classes, socialization, post-orphanage accommodation, we buy buggies, nappies, train young mothers, and sadly bury the ones we lose. We dress up what we do for grants and use fancy language when it is required by donors, and indeed we do have every detail of every child's life carefully mapped, and we do every single thing we can to make their sad, miserable existences warmer. But call it what you like – in a nutshell, what we do is provide a drop of warmth in their cold, lonely, sad world, and we are honoured to stand side by side with good Russian people while we do this.

Institutions, whether past or current, are simply not suitable places for children. Children need their mother's love, family, hugs, kisses, encouragement. We are all aware of the science. You need to breath confidence into them as babies so they will grow up strong and confident themselves, and go forward as functioning adults and parents in their turn.

Institutions cannot do this. It is not possible, so yes, the EU have it right – let's close them all, President Putin and his administration agree, thankfully, and the scene has been set to do this. All orphanages have to change to "family type orphanages." Fosterers are being trained to take the children – some are good, some bad, most are not properly trained yet as it is such early days – and for the first time I am hearing Russians talking about keeping the babies with their own mamas and strengthening those very mamas.

This is the only way forward.

Children are emotionally raped repeatedly in institutions all over the world. Really, the change is too slow in Russia but the numbers are so big. I have consciously avoided places full of handicapped and broken children, as I knew they would take me to my knees. I am an ordinary mum, an ordinary wife, and I know I could not cope with these ones, I felt I could never make a difference. I take my hat off to people like our own Avril Conroy who does huge work in Russia, Fiona Corcoran from Cork, organisations like Diema's Dream, who care for severely disabled children in some of the Russian institutions. These people do this work daily and without ego. We are not good at this type of care, we are too ordinary, but we have our arms full of children, abandoned, lonely, broken-hearted, weeping for their mamas, and we mind them well. We love them as much as possible, and we get them through the terrible system they are stuck in.

I think I am slowly beginning to understand the Russian psyche. It only took me a decade and a half, but as their own poet Fyodor Tyutchev said, "you cannot understand Russia with your mind, you can only believe in Russia." I am in his camp for sure!

Why do Russian mothers give up their babies and never come back to visit? I have asked myself this question a thousand times over the past 16 years. I used to be so angry at this, but I have watched so many children arriving and now I have a better picture. We are still living with the legacy left after 80 years of Communism, where the State was God. If the mama is poor or drinking, traditionally, maternity houses would take her baby from her, the mama would be told that her child will be well reared by the State and the mama was no longer required, and not encouraged to visit, ever. President Putin inherited a huge problem. When he came to power, babies were being taken from birth mothers in their hundreds of thousands and an adoption pipe was flowing to the west – with huge funds changing hands in some cases (not all), just like our own Irish babies being sold off to Americans, as we are hearing now from Bessborough and the like. This whole situation is being addressed now by the Russians; it is all under review.

To Russia With Love do not do adoptions, we have never done one although many Irish have asked us to help as there is practically no help in Ireland being offered to them. We don't help, it is not our area, and anyway I have been specifically told not to offer advice or assistance. The Irish government have made a total mess of adoption at home; many couples have suffered, and many children have been deprived of wonderful families. I try to stay out of this area, plus there are wonderful Irish people fighting this battle with our government, people desperate to offer their homes, their lives and their love to children languishing in institutions all over the world – often they are wasting their time.

Some of our Irish civil servants in Russia have done their best to progress adoption, and an odd one at home cares – a very odd one – but in general there is no willingness in Ireland at the top to encourage foreign adoption. They have never been brave enough to say they are against it, and as a result many couples are strung along, and totally stressed out as a result. Many of them call us, usually in floods, or for some kind of advice. Our side is quite horrendous to them, in my opinion.

Russians like to think that their institutions are fine places where the inmates should be grateful for carefully-rationed food, cheap clothing, eked-out shampoo and where sanitary towels are considered a luxury. In reality, they are mostly not fine places – some are wonderful, when you get a good director, but they are the rare ones.

Baby orphanages are always clean, good places, but when the children move on the bigger institutions at the age of six, they are past the age where they are likely to be adopted, and the standards drop. Huge buildings, massive maintenance issues, brutal winters, provincial staff, good and bad directors. We Irish know this story well, because we were very similar, and not so very long ago. Maybe we were even worse, if you listen to the tribunals.

There is still a strange attitude at work in Russia as people turn away. They don't want to hear the cries from over the orphanage walls, but then neither did we. It is easier just not to listen to them.

Given what happened here in Ireland not too long ago, I believe we are in no position to pass judgment on any other country. The boy in *White on Black* had a Spanish mother and a Russian father, and so was berated every day by some orphanage staff on the basis

"I have met many incredible people in Russia who are good, measured, experienced and caring; who know how to make a difference. These are the voices that need listening to."

that his mother was a 'black-assed bitch". Ireland was just the same – look at Christina Buckley's story, listen to her talking about the beatings little ones got for nothing other than being illegitimate. She herself had 100 stitches after one beating from her carers, and the doctors and nurses who stitched her back together sent her back to Goldenbridge, to the very women who had beaten her. We stand as a nation ashamed, and if we don't, we should. Too many children were and are incarcerated and punished for the errors of their parents.

In Ireland, historically the Church controlled these institutions, and dare you comment! In Russia the State does, and similarly, not enough people comment. People are too busy getting on with their own lives, too busy to hear the cries of the children or, in the case of so many orphanages, no cries at all, because the children have learned that crying does no good, no one is listening.

My mother lived in the last house in Celtic Park in Dublin 9; there were only fields between her back garden and the Artane Boys Industrial school. When the ragged little army of Artane boys were out walking in the fields 70 years ago, the family children on my mother's road had to look away. They were told not to even look at those boys as they were so bad. Now of course we know they were nothing of the sort, they were victims of a disgusting system. These huge systems take decades to change. Thankfully we have good people in Ireland now sorting out our mess, the people chosen for our new Department of Children and Family Services would give me hope. I hope people like Gordon Jeyes and Eibhlin Byrne will make change happen. Ministers come and go far too often.

If I can beam myself into a time warp, which I do every time I enter our orphanages, then I feel I can intervene where my mother could not. My Russian world is like Ireland was when we had orphanages. Thankfully we do not have to deal with the Catholic Church in Russia – its abuses, sex scandals, lies and cover ups – but we have other stuff to deal with. We are needed and, I am proud to say, welcomed in Russia. Of that there is no doubt. I am very grateful that we have such access, I admire the Russians so much for allowing this, including Ambassador Peshkov and his team, their door is always open. I doubt the Irish would have allowed it; they had too much to hide. Very few got past Mother Superior's office.

The numbers still in institutions in Russia are huge, as we are living with the legacy of the Soviet Union, when the State itself created a system where people felt it was acceptable to leave your child to be raised in an institution rather than in the arms of a family. This is where the mistake was made, now Russia and Mr Putin's team are trying to reduce the massive numbers they inherited. It is a slow task, very slow, and some unsuitable answers are being found. But I have met many incredible people in Russia who are good, measured, experienced and caring; who know how to make a difference. These are the voices that need listening to.

I am lucky to work with many of these great Russian people – people who care, who want to see change, who welcome us with open arms, who bestow medals upon us, who care deeply for the children, who are magnificent human beings. But, as with every path in life, I also work with cold, heartless people who should not have the jobs they have. This is life everywhere, not just Russia.

We know we should be clever and only focus on foster care, not on supporting the big old institutions behind those walls, tucked away in poor villages, lost in huge forests but I, for one, am staying behind the walls. For as long as there are children there, I will still be at their bed at night, kissing and tucking them in, and walking with them along every step of their tragic, lonely existence, because that is what my gut tells me to do. If I do say it myself, we are great at it.

We have a wonderful team, I get all the medals, but the entire To Russia With Love team are just incredible people and do most of the work that I get most of the credit for.

Some orphanage children will never find homes to love them, and as long as no one else wants those children, I make no apologies for the fact that we will stick by them whether this is seen as un-PC and anti-EU policy or not.

> "I am so proud of our children and never as much as I am now having read the stories that they have given to this book."

I am so proud of our children and never as much as I am now having read the stories that they have given to this book. Although we have changed the names of the younger ones, for the sake of discretion, the pages ahead are exactly their words. The stories they tell are raw, tragic, and inspiring. The stories you are about to read are not specific to Russia, they are the same as stories of children all over the world who have been abandoned to poverty and a loveless existence. These children have to climb mountains to get to where 'normal' is; family children do not have this climb to struggle with every day.

I would like to thank them all for the pain they must have felt recounting their past. Yet they all wanted to tell their story, they want to share the pain, and we are more than happy to listen if it relieves one drop of their sadness. I hope you are as moved by their stories as we all are. We are broken hearted for them and they know we are. They are the heroes of this whole Irish-Russian tapestry. They have fought and survived the horrors of their tragic backgrounds, inflicted on them by their parents, family and State.

There is no doubt Russia saved us all in the West from the ravages of Hitler in World War II. Stoic, brave and resilient, 26 million of them died and changed the path of history for us all, a fact most of us give little consideration to. We would have nothing in the West without the bravery of their heroes. In fact we owe our freedom to them. Now I am lucky enough to be working with another generation of heroes, just smaller ones.

The following pages explain why you help us. We give these children back self-worth, We build their damaged self esteem in a myriad of ways. We are a small drop of warm water on the layers of ice that have covered up their hearts. Nothing heroic, nothing extraordinary. In fact, we couldn't be more ordinary. We are just filling a gap, until they get sorted.

That's us.

Dublin, October 2014

How did I get here?

I t's early morning in Hortolova. The children are in
school and the playground is
empty. Spring has come
finally and the snow has melted,
leaving behind the usual winter
damage. Paintwork on the buildings is cracked and peeled. They
should be repainted – we used to
repaint every spring after the
ravages for six months of snow
and ice – but we don't have the
budget for that any more.

Continued on next page

Debbie with some of the
children in the Hortolova
playground in 2014. "By now,
after 16 years of constant
visits, constant
engagements, I know this
place as well as my own
house, my own back
garden."

The air is clear and pure, with a faint tang of pine, and overhead is the sound of a woodpecker tap-tap-tapping against a tree trunk.

In a couple of hours, this clearing will be full of children, playing football, in the playground, chatting, laughing, chasing the orphanage dog. Inside, the orphanage staff, those employed by the State as well as by To Russia With Love, some who were once children in this very orphanage, grown into fine young people, will be waiting with the many queries, requests, observations and problems that are generated by 100-odd children living under one roof, without family or friends in the outside world.

By now, after 16 years of constant visits, constant engagements, I know this place as well as my own house, my own back garden. I know the smells and rhythms of the day, the needs of the children, the problems of the staff, and – especially recently – the constant fear around where the next funds are coming from, and what will happen to these children if we don't raise the money.

But how did I get here? And why do I keep coming back? I am still sometimes taken by surprise at the events that overtook my life and led me here.

I published a book two years ago telling the story of how I first came to Russia and what I found here. Now, in this book, I want to tell the stories of the children we have helped during the last 16 years. Who they are, where they come from, why they end up with no one except a handful of Irish to care for them, and what their lives hold. These stories are the reason why I cannot walk away.

First, I will re-tell my own story, for those readers who don't know it. And for those of you who do, who have perhaps read my first book, feel free to skip ahead to the children's stories.

In 1997 my husband and I were parents to two young children. Sophie was seven, Mikey was three. We lived a pleasant, modest existence in Clontarf, where my life was made up of trips to school and Montessori, coffee with the other mums, shopping, cooking, and the usual domestic duties.

We weren't rich for sure, but we felt we had enough and with Mikey at playschool in the mornings, I had space in my life for a new challenge. At the time, taking orphans from Chernobyl for the summer was a big thing among kindly Irish families. We were told that by taking these children in for couple of weeks, feeding them, caring for them and letting them breath fresh air, you gave them two extra years of life – largely untrue but we all wanted to believe it; nice marketing always works.

So Mick and I decided to take two little girls, Zina and Valya, both seven years old. The day arrived, and off we went to the airport to collect these two tiny, undernourished little things, with head lice and threadbare clothes. In the car on the way home, Zina leaned forward and put a hand on Mick's shoulder. 'Papa?' she asked. It was the most heartbreaking question in the world, and neither Mick nor I trusted ourselves to give any kind of answer. That was the beginning of a very special bond between Zina and Mick that was to last for many years, and the start for both him and me of the feeling that we couldn't send these girls back to whatever sad and lonely place they had come from.

We had never intended to adopt a child, the idea had never once crossed our minds, but it somehow became unthinkable not to. As we got to know the girls, and began to work out what must be the contrast between their lives and the lives of our own adored children – and how little we knew back then! – the prospect of returning them to the orphanage became impossible. The girls were thin, silent, neglected, with worryingly low energy levels, painful boils, and the closed-in mentality that comes from being brought up in an institution.

No matter how many times we showed them the bowl of fruit in the middle of the table, or how to open the fridge, telling them in our very basic Russian to help themselves if they were hungry, they couldn't physically do it. They just didn't understand the concept. Children in orphanages never see a fridge – food arrives at mealtimes, is handed to them, they eat what they are given, and that's that. To them, helping themselves felt like stealing. To watch these two little girls gradually transform over the summer into more open, trusting, playful children, to see

> "After abandoning their children, or having them removed, these mothers and fathers only very rarely come back and visit. They may write once or twice, but rarely much more than that and often not at all."

them responding to the pantomime of goodwill that came from Sophie and Mikey, and start to behave a little more like Irish children, a little less like the terrified inmates of institutions that they had been, was a profoundly moving experience. I saw then just what a change love and kindness can bring about.

At the time, I believed these Russian orphans were all like Oliver Twist – the product of two tragically dead parents. Bit by bit I began to learn that the truth is even more tragic – most Russian orphans have at least one living parent, often two. But these parents are either unable or refuse to look after them. Alcohol and drugs are huge problems, particularly alcohol, with many of society's poorest and least educated taking to drink in a way that leaves them incapable of caring for their children, who become so neglected – starved, beaten, often forced out into the streets, badly dressed, exposed to dysfunctional behaviour from the adults around them –

that eventually the State intervenes and removes the children. That or the parents simply abandon them to State care, in the belief that the State will do a better job of raising them. And sometimes, when I hear the background stories of these children, I know that, for all that the State cannot provide love, or care, or cherish the children as they deserve, the parents were right; the State is the lesser of two great evils.

After abandoning their children, or having them removed, these mothers and fathers only very rarely come back and visit. They may write once or twice, but rarely much more than that and often not at all. They almost never feature in their children's lives again. Russian people tell me this is a legacy of Communism – that people genuinely believe the State will do a better job – but I still don't understand why they can't visit occasionally? Or write? Why they must break their children's hearts again and again by repeated failures of care and love? Invariably, despite the terrible things done to them, these children still love their mothers and long for contact. Knowing their parents are still out there, somewhere, means that they keep hoping, against all the odds, that one day someone will come back and claim them. In most cases, no one ever does.

Zina had lived in an orphanage since the age of 18 months, because her birth mother wasn't able to look after her. Her father later died, and her mother disappeared into one of the vast Russian forests, where she lived in a village made up of small wooden houses with a bunch of alcoholics, like something out of a crazy old fairytale, with no electricity, cut off from proper roads and civilization. These remote villages are not like anything we can imagine in Ireland. Picturesque on the one hand, but more often than not they have a dark side.

Of course Mick and I didn't know any of that at first. All we knew is that we couldn't send this child back. We didn't know then exactly what she was going back to, but we knew it wasn't a warm, loving family. So we decided to keep her. Valya, by the way, was also adopted by an Irish family and is now a beautiful, capable mother to little Emily, her sweet six-year-old.

I told the host organization who had brought in these summer-stay children that we had decided to hold on to one of the girls. Naturally, they thought I was being ridiculous, and told me, 'oh you'll settle down at the end of the month. You'll be delighted when its time for them to go back!' They presumed this was a case of 'puppy for Christmas' syndrome, that I was having an emotional reaction, and would regret my decision. They had a point, because that can certainly happen. Moved by the plight of a child, decent people make snap decisions, which they later regret bitterly when they learn how difficult and damaged these children can be. However, in our case, the instinct Mick and I had to hold onto Zina wasn't wrong. We really did have a deep bond, despite the initial language difficulties.

Why did we decide to keep her? Frankly, we didn't think it through; we acted on instinct. I tend to work with what my gut tells me, and if something feels right, I do it. Keeping Zina felt right. She herself said, from very early on, 'I'm not going back!' and we respected that. Also, I knew we could take on her problems – I wasn't so naïve that I couldn't see that a child who has lived seven years in an institution will have all sorts of difficulties – but I knew myself and my family, and I knew we could manage it.

Keeping Zina here was a battle that was to take over much of our lives for the next five years. Adoption in this country was – still is – a ridiculous process, and the kinds of hoops they forced us to jump through still make me angry when I think about it. However, crucially, unlike other couples trying to adopt, Mick and I already had our child, and no one would have been allowed to take her away – although the Eastern Health Board, (now the HSC) did at first try to tell us that we would have to send Zina back to Russia, spend five years getting approval, and only then go and get her. I told them pretty quickly where they could go with that idea – which meant that, ridiculous as the whole process was, we could at least get on with our lives, with Zina, in the meantime.

The Irish had no solutions as we did not fit in their box so I took myself off to the Russian Embassy here in Ireland, to tell them what was going on, and ask for their help and support, which they most generously gave. They did a deal with me – as long as I agreed that they could call, unannounced, at any time, to our house, to Zina's school or to her doctor's, they would let her stay. We said yes, of course, and then had endless hilarious situations in which we tried to appear the perfect family, usually in the teeth of normal Irish domestic chaos, as successive senior Russian diplomats and their wives turned up unexpectedly at our front door. My mother was down every week with Brasso for the door knob, and that was when she wasn't in town buying me tablecloths! The grass in the front garden went from random cuts to Wimbledon-style lawns.

Looking back, that decision – to keep this little girl, to try to give her the loving family life she had never known – started both Mick and I on a long, difficult, often frustrating journey, one that changed our lives completely, and the lives of our children, as well as the lives of many Russian children and Irish adults.

Some months into our new life with Zina, she started to learn real English, and we were finally able to communicate with her, beyond the basic language of hugs and physical affection. That's when she began to talk to us about the children she had left behind, her classmates from the orphanage. She talked on and on about these kids, particularly a boy called Pasha, whose photo she kept beside her bed. I didn't fully understand it at the time, but the bond between those children is very intense. Without adults to love and protect them, they sometimes find these things among each other, forging very deep relationships in place of family. With Zina and Pasha, that's what it was like.

I only really understood all this years later, but I did get that Zina had a seven-year history with the children from her orphanage, and that I had simply lifted her out of that life. I could see this was disruptive and confusing for her, and that she was worried that her classmates in Russia wouldn't know what had happened to her. So I promised her that I would go to Russia, find those children and tell them that she was ok. I really had no other plan.

"I promised her that I would go to Russia, find those children and tell them that she was ok. I really had no other plan."

Looking back, I still can't believe how naïve and ignorant I was, and how totally unprepared for what had been the realities of Zina's life before we took her in. We knew she came from a remote children's home but certainly I had no idea what an orphanage looked like.

It was very difficult even to find the orphanage. Russian orphanages tend to be buried in the middle of deep woods, far from any towns or cities. But thanks to my Russian friends, I tracked down the place where Zina's classmates had been transferred from the baby orphanage where she had lived with them. The new orphanage was called Hortolova, in a region called Bryansk, which borders Ukraine and Belarus, and when I first heard the word, I had no idea what it would come to mean in my life.

The shock of Hortolova

I made a decision to find out where she was from and so myself and a close friend flew to Minsk from Shannon, then travelled another nine hours by car through Belarus before getting to the Russian border. Finally, I walked through the gates of this overgrown, dilapidated, forgotten place, like a derelict factory, where the grass grew higher than the windows and hordes of children were massing everywhere, without purpose or direction that I could see. It was like walking into a different world, or even a different century, somewhere wild and forgotten. It was September, a beautiful month in Russia, but very cold, and nothing in this place was beautiful.

The heating was broken and a bitter wind whistled through the broken windowpanes. The children were dirty, wearing cheap, plastic shoes that had holes in them and certainly didn't keep the cold out. Many of them had no jackets. The kitchens were filthy, with the kind of deep, ingrained dirt that seems to have been laid down over years, and there wasn't a single working toilet for 200 children.

The boys' block smelled like the lion's enclosure at the zoo – that overpowering urine smell – and the boys were simply shitting on the ground of the bathrooms. The girls were cleaner about themselves, although their toilets weren't working either. I just couldn't believe the conditions these children were living in. The dormitories were huge, filled with jangly old steel beds, like a military hospital, with great piles of dirty clothes everywhere, and dogs sleeping on them. There were piles of filthy clothes up to the ceiling in the laundry room. The smells everywhere were disgusting. The children themselves were filthy; the hardest thing for me to deal with, frankly, were their teeth – none of them had ever seen a toothbrush, let alone a dentist, and all their teeth were covered in a kind of greenish gunk. It was tough sometimes not to recoil in disgust at the sight.

Times were brutally hard all over Russia in 1998, as their economy had just crashed and many millions were living in terrible poverty. Yeltsin was on the way out, no one was coping with capitalism after decades of Communism, wages had not been paid in months. It was not a good time to be an ordinary civilian, never mind an orphan, who are bottom of the social ladder at the best of times. Hortolova back then was a terrible place. One little girl, a tiny little slip of a thing, had the shape of an iron burned onto her face, as though she had been branded. Sadly, bullying is endemic in these institutions, and often the carers do little to protect small, vulnerable children from the older ones.

Worse even that the physical hardship was the fact that no one seemed to be minding these children. There was no sign of anyone in charge, although strange old men wandered freely around. We didn't know who they were, or what they were doing, but it all felt incredibly unprotected. I was bowled over by the danger of it, and stunned that we were so close to Europe. There I was, in my lovely warm jacket, inappropriately holding bags of sweets that I had brought for the children. I couldn't believe how naïve and stupid I felt. The last things these children needed was sweets or stupid clueless visitors.

I walked through the buildings in a stunned silence. In one of the huge dormitories, a girl was lying in her bed, sobbing. She was bruised all over, black and blue. Via our interpreter, I asked, what's wrong with you? She told us that one of the boys had beaten her, so I went and found the boy, and read him the riot act. I told him never to raise a hand to a girl again, how dared he, and so on. I must have thought I was going to solve all the problems of the world in one week. It was ridiculous. But to Sasha, the girl who had been beaten, I was her saviour. She held my hand for the entire week I was there, and when it came time for us to leave, she didn't want to let me go. I had my arms around her, saying good-bye, and she said to our interpreter – 'tell Debbie I've never been kissed before.' She was nine years old.

> "One little girl, a tiny little slip of a thing, had the shape of an iron burned onto her face, as though she had been branded."

Until then, I had never intended to come back. I had found Zina's classmates – all except Pasha, who had inspired this mission in the first place, but who wasn't there – had given them all sweets and a letter from her, and made some vague promises. I intended to pack a bag of toys once I got home, maybe some old clothes, and send them out. But Sasha wasn't letting me go. I was crying, she was crying. And that comment of hers just broke me. It hit me like a ton of bricks, along with the misery and neglect all around us. It also made me realise that I could do something; I thought, "well, I can't fix the place, and I can't rebuild this old building, but I can come back and hug this child."

And so I made her a promise. "I will come back, and I will kiss you and hug you on your birthday."

Little did I know that this promise, lightly made, would be one I was still carrying out 16 years later.

As I said goodbye to Sasha and the other children on that cold

September day, they all crowded around us, begging us to stay and even barred the gates to stop us leaving. I had no idea that this promise of mine – to come back – would mean that 16 years later I would still be trying to keep faith with the children of Russia's orphanages.

I had made my promise to Sasha, and I sobbed all the way home. I had a complete meltdown. Suddenly Zina, who I was used to feeling so sorry for, seemed to have so much, because these children had literally nothing. They were living in squalor, with meagre food, no treats, no playgrounds, no toys, nothing to cheer or brighten their days. It was unbearable to me as a very ordinary Irish mother, but fixable somehow, I just was not sure yet how.

When doing nothing is not an option

Once home, I think I sat at the kitchen table in a daze for about a week, crying most of the time. I decided to have a fund-raising coffee morning, supported by some great women and cake-bakers – just like a typical Irish housewife! We raised about £7000 that day, partly because we added whisky to the coffee! It was huge money for day one. We equipped a convoy – trucks carrying donated clothes, toys, food, blankets and so on – and I spent most of the funds on bringing out a doctor, Trisha McGrath who was a nurse, two builders from Electric Aid, John Mulligan, an experienced humanitarian and a journalist, Mary O'Sullivan, from the *Sunday Independent*. The plan was a fact-finding mission – find out how much needed to be done, realistically – and try and get a story into the paper to help us raise more money to do it.

So this team of us went out, in November when the temperature was minus 30 degrees Celsius. I think at the time I still thought this could be a quick fix – a six-month job fixing up the orphanage, then back to my life. I was utterly naïve about the can of worms I was opening, and the level of emotional engagement I was letting myself in for.

We did a big week at the orphanage, a full assessment of what the place needed. At the same time, even though we didn't yet have funds, I began talking to the Department of Education in Bryansk about the possibility of coming back and renovating the building block by block. Their attitude was that if we wanted to come back with building and childcare experts, they would happily work with us.

They weren't going to put any money into the project themselves – they didn't have it to spare – but they wouldn't hinder us, as long as we behaved with due consideration and respect. That was the beginning of what has been an invaluable and fruitful relationship, without which we could never have managed so much.

Dr Mark Wheeler and Trisha McGrath, my right arm at the time and for many years to come, examined the children and diagnosed something called psycho-social deprivation – through lack of love, they weren't growing. They were much smaller than the national average. A recent report indicated that even now, although conditions are much improved, every five months, children in Russian orphanages fall one month behind in average weight and growth. Back then, our doctor likened it to a plant without enough water; they were getting basic food requirements but only the bare minimum, and no love, so they simply couldn't thrive normally.

They also had head lice and signs of scabies, in fact many of them were raw with it. But the main problems were neglect, lack of love, lack of attention and of course the endless grinding poverty that is part of life for the majority of rural-dwelling Russians. It wasn't just these orphan children who were living in squalor and deprivation – the local villages were almost as bad, although we didn't see or notice that at first, because we were so overwhelmed by what needed to be done for the children.

That second trip was an incredible experience for us all. There was a lot of hysterical laughing, a lot of hysterical tears. We were all on a monstrous learning curve, we really had no idea how we were going to chew what we had bitten off. My head was spinning with the extent of what was needed. The question was, what on earth do you do with an orphanage in another country that's falling down? I hadn't a clue. I didn't know where to start. Do you knock it down? Fix it up? Ideally we should have been knocking it down and starting residential care, but it was too soon in Russia to do that – the country simply wasn't ready. There were no possibility of finding homes for these orphans, with more coming all the time, so we needed to do something else. Our plan was to try and renovate the orphanage to make it into a safe, warm, homely place, with smaller, brighter rooms and better facilities. Make it more like a home and less like a rundown old factory. Back in 1998, I had no better solution. It was -30 outside and there was no glass in most of the windows, or working central heating. We needed to get the children through the winter, and there just wasn't a different plan.

> "Back home, I somehow blustered my way onto Kenny Live, telling them 'I'm a housewife from Clontarf, and I need to talk to Ireland.'"

Back home, I somehow blustered my way onto *Kenny Live*, telling them 'I'm a housewife from Clontarf, and I need to talk to Ireland.'

To his great credit, Pat Kenny let me do it. Zina sat in the front row of the audience with her lovely sister Sophie, my husband, and the crew that had travelled, and I explained what I had found in Russia, and what I wanted to do about it. I think our ordinariness hit a nerve with many people, and for anyone who missed it, the *Sunday Independent* had a double page spread the next morning, with Mary O'Sullivan's first article, and Dave Conachy's fabulous photos of the children. It was a double whammy, and it began to yield results almost immediately.

Money started to pour in, small donations from regular people, and large donations – I remember we got $25,000 from one man the Monday morning after the *Sunday Independent* article – from the wealthy. The Celtic Tiger had just taken off, and there were men's lunches, ladies' lunches, auctions and charity balls galore. We were in the right place at the right time, and we reaped the rewards of the nation's prosperity and generosity. I came home one day shortly after *Kenny Live*, to find an envelope containing £20 stuck to my door, 'To Russia, With Love' scrawled across the front left by a beautiful friend of mine, Ann Delaney. Right there, the charity name was established.

The strength of the board

We set up a tiny office, and I formed a board, made up entirely of parents from my local area, even though my accountant was telling me to be strategic, to find a shrewd businessman, a consultant or a solicitor, for example, all of whom would have provided different fields of expertise. However my gut feeling was to ask friends of mine, people who were driven to help by the desire to mind and protect children.

All of those people are still patrons of the charity, and are all still very close friends. I am surrounded by a wonderful board of sensible, clever – doers – no bullshit, no expenses, no egos, all just people who care about children and watch over me.

We registered the charity immediately in Ireland and set up a bank account in Dublin, and from the very beginning we have had a clear paper trail of every single donation – every penny given. We have been unbelievably, painfully transparent, which has been hard, but well worth it. We can show chapter and verse on exactly where every penny is spent. In fact we opened our office, and our books of the past 16 years to a team of independent accountants this year. To be honest, I felt sick about it in case they saw something that we had not, but we got a glowing report published in a national newspaper. The headline read: "We searched to see if she ever travelled first class, she didn't." We are the McVities crew, there is no doubt of that.

The reason we offered to do that was to combat some of the damage caused to us all from the horrendous publicity of Rehab and the Central Remedial Clinic (CRC). Irish people needed to know that some of us do what we do properly and transparently, without huge salaries, pensions or expenses, and with passion.

There was so much practical stuff to be done, so much renovating and rebuilding and cleaning and mending, that at times it was hard to remember the other side of our mission – to love the children. To show them kindness, affection and respect, to try and build their self-esteem, something that is in very short supply with orphan children. To try and foster this, as well as proper bedrooms, clean new bathrooms, birthdays, menu choices etc, we built something that I called the suitcase room.

We had spotted the children going up and down a rickety ladder to this filthy old attic. One day I went up to see what they were doing, and found a room wedged with ancient old suitcases, mostly made out of battered cardboard. The children were like mice, scrabbling round at the suitcases, so I asked, 'what is this room?' It turned out that when the children first arrived to the orphanage, they brought with them a suitcase, which was then taken from them. They could have had an old pair of shoes in the case, or possibly a photo of their mother, or even a letter. These dirty, battered old suitcases were treasure trunks for these children, the only link with family and early life, but they were just dumped in the attic by staff, on top of one another, in great heaps. It was filthy, freezing and wet up there, with water running down the walls and snow falling through the broken roof. And yet these children would spend their time up there, hunting through the piles to find their own memories. Clearly, these suitcases were just the most precious things in the world to them. So when we renovated, we built a suitcase room. Now, they all have their own spot, on nice white shelves, with sliding ladders so they can reach their suitcase. We have tables where they can sit and go through it all. I felt it was very important to them to be able to do that.

We took on volunteers, many of them, good men and women from across Ireland who had heard my story and wanted to help by coming to Russia and working with us. One man called me the night after Pat Kenny, Mairtin ODubhghaill, he is still by my side 16 years later and he is one of the kindest people in Ireland. The children adore him. On those first trips, we would work on nuclear energy all day, and finally tuck the children in at night, then crash. We were nearly all ordinary mothers and fathers, those of us who travelled out on the early trips, and all day long we would be surrounded by small children, neglected and traumatised, usually dirty, with head lice and ringworm, who needed care so badly. There was so much to do – organising, cleaning, setting up programmes and putting systems in place, playing with these children, loving them, sometimes just sitting quietly with our arms around a tiny child who might have recently been abandoned by her mother and was still heart-broken and bewildered. It was physically exhausting and emotionally draining. By 8 or 9 o'clock at night, all any of us wanted to do was go back to the hotel where we stayed, fall into bed or crawl into a bottle of vodka – I don't even like vodka, but I would swim in it in Russia in those days.

On one of the early visits, a volunteer who worked as a childcare expert for the Health Board came out with us. He spent time in the orphanage, examining everything, then wrote a report back to the To Russia With Love board. His advice was to walk away, on the basis that we couldn't possibly make a difference to children when there were so few of us on the ground. He said that we would be taking all this money out of Ireland, and that it wouldn't be doing any good, because we simply didn't have enough people to change the system. I badly needed him to endorse what I was doing, so when I read this report, I thought, 'bloody hell! I hope he's wrong, because we're not going to give it up!' I gave it to the Board, and we had some very sobering meetings about it, but we decided to battle on and just wrap our arms around as many children as we could, to try and help them, because what else could we do? It's been a battle from day one. Everything single thing we've managed to achieve has been a tremendous battle.

Powering up, battling on

We soon found there was no point giving out to the staff in the orphanages, who were nearly as miserable as the children. They were only doing what they were told, following the regulations that had been laid down for the care of orphan children decades ago, and never changed. They may have been initially surly and without imagination or much affection in their handling of the children, but there was little else they could do under the circumstances. To really effect change, I needed to go above their heads, to where the real power was.

My first meeting with a Governor of Bryansk was exactly like the scene in the *Wizard of Oz* where Dorothy gets an audience with the wizard. The doors into the Wizard's office are 100ft high, down corridors that are kilometres long, and it's exactly the same in Russia; the further you walk, the smaller you feel. Its part of a whole pompous show, designed to make you believe the wizard is real, and intimidate anyone at a lower level. I've never seen bigger tables than those in Russian offices, so big you can fit 35 armchairs around them. There were usually soldiers with guns standing out the front, and legions of minions all bowing and scraping to the governor. All my Russian interpreters were extremely uncomfortable by the sheer scale of things, but for me, it was just the same as having some little man hiding behind the curtains, working the levers. I loved the drama of it.

> "When I told him his orphanages were a bloody disgrace, my interpreters were all horrified at my nerve, but he actually responded like a caring human being."

And yet, I found that once I got face-to-face with the governor, despite the soldiers, secretaries and assistants, he was after all only human. When I told him his orphanages were a bloody disgrace, my interpreters were all horrified at my nerve, but he actually responded like a caring human being, and was prepared to work with us, and allow us to spend the money we had raised on making life better for these children.

That said, the good sense of my interpreters and guides – in particular Igor Stepanov, who came on board almost on Day One of To Russia With Love, and has been my interpreter, guide, advisor, protector and friend ever since – did save me from a lot of ignorant blunders. At some of my first meetings, when I would be ranting about the awful conditions in the orphanages, these interpreters made the unilateral decision simply not to translate for me! Recently, I looked back at one of the TV3 documentaries, made in the very early days, at a scene in which I'm saying to a high-up Russian official, "I cannot believe the state the orphanages are in, this is disgusting and inhumane ...!" Now that I speak a bit of Russian, I can see that Igor, my wonderful interpreter, is conveying this, cautiously as "Debbie feels the conditions could be better..."

At the time, there were about 200 children in Hortolova, everything from sweet little six-year-old girls up to 18-year-old boys who looked like they'd knife you. These boys had been institutionalised all their lives and some were very aggressive. Hortolova, I later learned, had been formed only a year earlier – essentially from the unwanted children of other orphanages. The most difficult, demanding children, or those with the most complicated paperwork, from all over the region, had been taken out of other orphanages, because they were getting too big, and put together in this terrible place. The authorities simply opened this ancient, dilapidated building and filled it with children who were aggressive, or withdrawn, or who may have been sexually abused, or had never attended school. Essentially the children who needed extra care and attention were just dumped here and forgotten about.

Many of these children had significant problems, rooted in the neglect and abandonment of their early years. Psychologists call it an attachment wound, and it's like a big, black gaping hole at the centre of a child's being. It's a wound they will try to fill with anything – stealing, telling lies, bullying, forcing people to hate you. Low self-esteem is a classic symptom, as is addiction in later life. Some children suffer more than others, some don't manifest it until they are adults. But every one of our children was suffering to some degree from an attachment wound, and our mission was to help them overcome it, to heal it with the first unconditional love most of them had ever known.

The team for the long haul

We quickly gave up doing convoys, because the stuff, if it was any good, would come in the front door and go straight out the back. Thieving was a huge problem at the start. Instead, we realised that it was a much better idea to bring in money, and spend it in Russia. By contributing to the local economy and buying Russian items for the children, we reduced the amount of resentment felt by the villagers, and made it less likely that the stuff would simply be stolen.

I was very lucky early on to meet the assistant governor of Wheatfield Prison, an amazing man, who became my mentor, travelling companion, psychiatrist and friend. He was a true-blue civil servant, someone who understood the system and how to make it work. He taught me how to do what I needed to do, how to make things happen in Russia, he was one of many incredible people that lent me their shoulders to stand on. Without him, and many others – mainly my incredible husband and mother – there is no way I could have done what I did.

For example, in Russia, orphanage regulations were laid out

many decades ago, and are rigid and almost unchangeable. This kind of thing was incredibly frustrating for me, because I wanted to change everything now, now, now! Clean kitchens, working toilets, toys, good food, warm shoes … and wheels just don't turn like that in Russia, they grind slowly. Derek Tracy from Wheatfield prison trained us all in what was needed to get an institution from the lowest level up to something that we could find acceptable. There is a huge similarity between orphanages and prisons – except our children have committed no crime.

It took years, really, to start to see profound change in the children. Whatever the ditzy daytime TV presenters would have you believe, you cannot go into an orphanage, rebuild it in 24 hours, deliver a convoy, throw a bucket of paint over everything and a few teddy bears, and hope to make a difference. It absolutely doesn't work. It takes a huge amount of work, passion, time, energy, and patience.

> "We needed people who would live in a grotty old flat in a freezing orphanage. Who would put up with grim conditions – skinny, hard beds, cockroaches, minus 25 degrees outside and no hot water in the shower."

We never made much of an impact on the ones who were quite grown up when we arrived. They left shortly afterwards, and their lives were only slightly improved. The ones who were little when we first came, six or so, are so far our most successful children, because they have received the most love, attention and money. It's not rocket science. To fix children, you need time and resources and wonderful people. Those of our children who have gone on to university or technical school, have qualified as skilled craftsmen, have successfully married and had children of their own – these are the ones we have had the most time with and who have benefited from the full extent of our programs.

And in truth, we couldn't have put more hours or effort into doing this. We felt the children deserved every single drop of energy we could put into them, even when we ourselves were dropping with exhaustion and completely over-emotional. When the core team wasn't there, our incredible Irish volunteer carers, who would go out on three-month programs, did it for us.

These carers came from all over the country, and from every kind of background, but they all had certain things in common – an extraordinary patience and kindness. We needed people who would live in a grotty old flat in a freezing orphanage. Who would put up with grim conditions – skinny, hard beds, cockroaches, minus 25 degrees outside and no hot water in the shower, and who would still be able to smile, hug, mind the children. Their job description was simply TLC. They were not there to teach, to feed, or to run the orphanage. The State staff continued to do all these things on a daily basis. Our volunteers were there to love those children, to play with them, to show them the kind of affection they had never known. They had to be self-motivating, because we didn't give them a structure. They had to be able to get up in the morning and do whatever the day demanded, and the children needed. If some child wanted to sit quietly beside you and hold their hand for an hour, their job was to be there. They had to take their lead from the kids – play football, sing, read, draw; whatever the children wanted.

Once the program was up and running, we had three or four carers going out every 12 weeks, and changing over with the team already there. It was a huge amount of maintenance – they lost their passports, got sick, got homesick, couldn't take any more cold water in the showers. Whatever it was, I was their link, so they would ring me if they were having a bad moment. They also rang if they had concerns about the children, any kind of bullying or abuse. Anything they saw that they didn't like – whether it was no petrol for the bus or the children not being allowed play with the toys we had brought them – five seconds later I would know about it. That was something I had to manage carefully. Older, Soviet Russians, raised in a different system, can be paranoid about Westerners being spies, and I couldn't let the State staff think these people were anything other than good people, so I had to be very careful about how I used the information. Once we gained the respect of the staff, and they realised we weren't reacting in a bitchy, malicious way, but only to improve the level of care, it became easier. My own children became part of this team as did Trisha's and others. Mikey and his friends did basketball camps, Sophie, like me, loves Russia, and loves many of our children like her own siblings. She has been there many times and many of the children have grown up with her by their side.

There were five or six carers living in the orphanage flat at any one time, and all day long, all they heard at the door was 'knock, knock, knock,' as children found any excuse they could to come and see them. We had around 200 children, and they would always find a reason to knock for the Irish. Carers might be having a quick tea break and a rest, and the next thing, 'knock-knock,' and some little kid is standing there, sometimes without any real reason. They'd make something up – 'I need a pencil, a plaster', anything at all. Or they'd forget what they wanted as the door opened, they just wanted to see a friendly warm smile. For 18 hours a day, it never ceased. The Irish never got tired of it, every single person we sent out was incredible. At one point the State Russian carers facilitated the Irish carers with a Weight Watchers class in our medical block as the Irish needed weighing in weekly due to over-consumption of waffles and bread. This was new to the Russians but the Irish needed it. A great bond was growing between us all. I loved this bond, it is one that has lasted for 17 years and has brought lovely people from across Ireland and across the world into my life.

Breaking the cycle of despair

We also began a system of sponsor families here in Ireland for our Russian children, and many wonderful, amazing Irish families came forward, and worked through Noreen Lyons to link with hundreds of children. These sponsor families donated €200 a year and, maybe more importantly, they wrote to the children: letters, birthday cards, Christmas cards, back and forth to Russia, all year long. Our children adore the letters. They wait for them, and all have a photo of their sponsor families beside their beds. When we go in and say goodnight to them, they will tell us all about the sponsor families – how so-and-so got a new cat, or a car or something. Often, they never actually meet these sponsor families, in fact, mostly they never meet them, but they still become very attached to them.

The children write back, and tell the families about their birthday gift, school, or a new haircut. Its very simple stuff, but it's a strong link, one they are very proud of. I remember one of our difficult children, Lena, and the difference made to her by the letters she received from her sponsor mother, who used to write to her endlessly, cheering her on and just chatting to her. Lena is with her in Ireland this year, and Emma has certainly saved this 21-year-old from prison, and worse. She has turned her into 'normal' – Lena was a far cry from 'normal' when we first got her aged six, but it has been a battle over many years to achieve this result.

We never turn our backs on the children. For as long as they need us, we're there. Even if they end up in prison. And yes, it has happened. But only once. Generally, we are unbelievably successful at keeping them out – when you consider that the national average for orphan boys who go on to prison is 30-odd percent – our record is remarkable. These boys tend to go from one institution to another, becoming rougher, more aggressive, more dysfunctional human beings along the way. There is no safety net to prevent this in Russia. No system to intervene and help these children, to stop them becoming the hopeless cases that endlessly perpetuate the vicious cycles. Our goal is to stop that self-perpetuating misery of orphans growing into aggressive, low-achieving adults, dropping through the social strata until they end up as dysfunctional alcoholics like their own parents, and putting their own children into State care, only for the whole awful thing to start again.

> "These boys tend to go from one institution to another, becoming rougher, more aggressive, more dysfunctional human beings along the way."

Our plan – and we are very good at it – is to break that cycle, to give them the self-esteem, the support, the belief they need to make a success of their lives. And I'm not talking about graduating from university as a doctor or lawyer – although we have those ones too. All we want for our children is a decent job, stable relationships, a sense of self-worth. This we instil in them via our many programs and the unconditional love we show.

How Did They Get Here?

For all that I have worked in Russia for 16 years, and seen again and again at first-hand the way in which Russian parents abandon their children, I still find it hard to understand.

I have tried rationalising what I know of the background to these sad stories, to try and create a picture of the social circumstances that lead to this tragic point of no-return, and that helps to give some kind of picture of the whys. But I am also very aware, and I never let myself forget it, that Ireland is very far from perfect in this regard. Many of the things I find so hard to accept about the Russian attitude towards orphans, dysfunctional families, vulnerable people in hardship and great need, are very similar to practices that were rampant in Ireland less than 50 years ago.

Ireland has a very bad record, and so we are in no position to lecture and condemn what happens in Russia. The best we can do is try to understand, and help where we can. Their country is essentially 20 years old, as Communism is not that long gone. Our country is 100 years old, and we're still saying we're a young country and using that as an excuse for our idiosyncrasies, our Craggy Island-ness, and the appalling treatment of women and children by church and state.

Alcohol – vodka, basically – is a huge social problem in Russia, and dirt cheap. What they are drinking, many of them, is rocket fuel, hooch. This stuff is gut rot. Brewing your own vodka is illegal in Russia, the same as it is in Ireland, but many farmers still make their own out of grain and potatoes, just as we brew poitin. So this home-brew can be bought anywhere, dirt cheap, and it can cause brain damage to those who drink it in large quantities. If the women are pregnant and drinking heavily, their babies can be affected too; 'oligrophenic' they call it, meaning a child who can't be educated, basically.

For women who fall pregnant and aren't married, who are poor and without much support, the usual option is a maternity house, where they go to have their babies. And there the nurses and doctors might encourage the mother to put the child into an institution, because they genuinely feel the institution will do a better job of raising the child – no more than we did here until not very long ago. These doctors and nurses are not judgmental or horrible necessarily, although some can be, but they have this mindset of State intervention and they rarely question this – if the State says the child is better in an institution, that's where they put the child. We are beginning to see changes at last in the maternity houses, with greater efforts made to keep mothers and babies together. However, there is a long way to go, and right now, the procedure is take the baby and the mother walks away. She gets no counselling, no nurturing, no last kiss on the head and book of photographs and memories, just a brutal tearing apart. Often, the mother can't cope with what she's done. She might turn to drink as a way to blot out the pain, alcohol becomes the easiest path, maybe ending up stealing shoes or bread, and going to prison. She never goes back to visit the child because the child is just a distant, painful memory. When Marian Keyes visited Hortolova with us six years ago, this is what she found so hard to deal with; it broke her heart actually.

Once we began digging behind the official files on our children, the truth contained within bald statements of fact: 'Mother an alcoholic, deprived of parental rights. Whereabouts of father unknown. Mother's current whereabouts unknown...' this is the kind of story we found far too often. Our children's family circumstances are like a cross-section of the worst things that could happen to a child: neglect, abandonment, violence, abuse, suicide, murder, drug abuse, alcoholism, mental illness. All these things feature with shocking, mind-numbing regularity. None of them is unique to Russia – these are the stories of poverty and ignorance all over the world. I am certain that looking hard enough at inner city Dublin would throw up similar images; it just happens that Russia is where I encounter them.

None of the children whose stories are contained in this book has been visited by their mother more than once or twice; most never. Sometimes – rarely – a father will come, more often it's a grandmother or an aunt, if indeed anyone comes, but almost never a mother.

By and large, the grandmothers are the lynchpins of rural Russian society. They are a different generation, they came through Communism and are used to having very little and working very hard. They have a strong idea of their place in the world, and of the need to keep going despite hardship. Capitalism didn't change their lives at all really, whereas their children absorbed ideas about freedom, wealth, luxury, that for them have never translated into reality. Money became a god and Russia has been gorging on it since Communism ended, but for the parents of our children, there is no trickle-down effect. They are poor Russians, they see no way out, except that now they know far more about what other people have in the West and in their own country too.

Russians can be very harsh to each other. In a country of 144 million, only the strong survive. If you look at successful middle-class Russians, they never stop trying to succeed. They work so hard, their children study so hard, they speak three or four languages fluently by their early teens, they push their kids far harder than we do, because in order to succeed, they have to be very well educated. The main focus is academic achievement. When they come to Ireland, say to work in the embassy, these Russians are horrified that their children only get an hour or two of homework at night; in Russia those kids would be up until 11.30 every night studying. These families are driven by a different mentality, one carved from communism, a complex history and by the need to get to the top or go under.

Families in Russia are small – one or two children – and these children are treated like the last Emperor. I'm starting to see it in Ireland too, as women have fewer children and later; the children are treated as though they are infinitely precious, nothing like the old days of nine to a family, where everyone had to scramble to survive. I think children were better for it, less spoiled, more mature, better able to cope with real life and its endless challenges.

Family is sacred in Russia, and within family circles, people are very good and trusting of each other. If a brother or cousin needs financial help, large or small, they will give it to him, almost with no questions asked. They will do anything to help those within the tight family circle, but the flip-side of that is that outside of the family circle, they don't trust easily.

Show them an orphanage 100-meters away from their house, and it may as well be invisible. Our orphans are in no-mans' land, and no man wants to know them. Locals don't give to orphanages, they don't walk in on a Sunday with a bag of sweets for the kids or even a few pairs of socks. I've been working in Bryansk for 16 years now and many other places across Russia, and I meet Russian people all the time who tell me, 'you're doing such wonderful work, it's so great what you do for Russia children,' but it doesn't occur to them to do anything themselves – even to pop out on a

Sunday with a bag of ice-pops, for example. They tell me I'm wonderful, but I don't inspire them to do the same. I suppose they are busy surviving and caring for their own families; so they don't have room in their lives to help others. Life can be so hard in Russia that there is no energy or emotion left over for other people. But, having said that, I doubt many people went through the doors of Bessborough in Cork, Letterfrack and our many other places packed with innocent children, with ice-pops on a Sunday. Possibly if more Irish had done this they would have sensed what was going on behind those walls

> "They will do anything to help those within the tight family circle, but the flip-side of that is that outside of the family circle, they don't trust easily."

sooner than they did. The situations are really not that different; the real difference is scale. In Ireland we had a few thousand children in institutions at any one time, in Russia that figure was 750,000 ten years ago, 150,000 now. Vladimir Putin, his governors and his administration's plan are inevitably slow, but they are finally working to eradicate these institutions.

In the meantime, we have too few visitors and not enough kindness shown to our children, by individuals or the State. 'Child-focussed' is the big buzz-word here now when dealing with any situation children find themselves in, whether bullying at school or family breakdown. But it is still a new word to us, and doesn't exist yet in Russia. There, when family structures break down, there is no support at all. No efforts are made to keep the family together, mediate or help in anyway. Here, somebody would intervene to support the child within the family, set up counselling sessions, therapy, mediation, but not there. The mother goes one way, the father goes the other, and the child goes into an orphanage. A big scary person arrives into the flat, scoops the child up and takes him or her away. No one explains to them what or why this is happening, they just take them. And the children do what they're told without asking questions, because they are children, and because all Russians do what they're told by authority, because they are frightened not to.

The first real social workers are only coming through the educational system in Russia now and it will be many years before change is seen. Putin is trying to bring in a more child-focussed approach, and it is starting to happen in small pockets. He has some great people working under him and they are our hope for change. The entire system is a massive wheel moving inch by inch, weighed down by bureaucracy, lack of money, indifference and set-in-their-ways civil servants.

One thing, strangely, we have not had to deal with much during the 16 years of To Russia With Love is sexual abuse. In our experience, there is more abuse perpetrated between children in orphanages, than that involving adults. That said, where there are vulnerable children and adults in authority without much check on them, there is certain to be abuse.

At the moment, many Russians believe that sexual debauchery and abuse only exist in the West; exactly as we used to think in this country – that it was an English or an American thing – until the appalling stories started to come out, and just kept coming. They have trained their nation to believe they don't have a lot of the problems the West has – that they may not have the same luxuries, but that they are better people; the idea of the corrupt West is a powerful one. And so, for many of them, sexual abuse of children is considered an impossibility, something that never happens.

In fact, we have seen little evidence of it, and we have looked. However, I think in 20 years time in Russia, it is very likely that the stories will start to pour out, just as they did here. The children who end up in orphanages have been so unprotected within their family situations, so profoundly neglected, that it seems impossible it should not have happened.

We have had very obvious cases of sexual abuse in some of the places we work in, although not many. The problem is, none of the psychologists in the region can cope with this, they aren't trained to deal with it, and so it is not identified except in the most obvious of cases. In the absence of clear information, all we can do is what we always do – our best to nurture and mind them and get them back on their feet. If they follow Ireland, many, many stories will be told in the future. Humans are the same everywhere and abusers are drawn to children's institutions, like moths to light.

I think our children in Hortolova feel safe and are safe, because we are there all the time, minding them, listening to them, watching over them. There is a spotlight on them and I think we've made them safe because of that. However, there is no doubt that before coming to us, they have all been abused; whether its physical, sexual or emotional, they have all suffered terrible abuse.

If you look at the UN Declaration of the Rights of the Child, it's such a beautiful thing – "The child … needs love and understanding. He shall, wherever possible, grow up in the care and under the responsibility of his parents … a child of tender years shall not, save in exceptional circumstances, be separated from his mother." "The child is entitled to receive education… He shall be given an education which will promote his general culture and enable him, on a basis of equal opportunity, to develop his abilities, his individual judgement, and his sense of moral and social responsibility, and to become a useful member of society." "The child shall be protected against all forms of neglect, cruelty and exploitation."

Our children don't have those rights. They grow up in a world where they are absolutely alone. I still wonder, looking at our children, how you get through life without love? Without comfort? Without kindness? Without somebody to rub your back when you're feeling low? I know it's their norm, but all the same they must have a terrifying feeling of falling off the edge of a cliff all the time. There is no safety net. That feeling of edgy nervousness, that hole in the middle of your stomach, they must feel it all the time. They must grow up with that feeling – because there is nothing between them and the abyss. Except us, and there aren't enough of us. We're strong, but we're small.

If funds dry up, what do we do with these children? It's so much easier to give to charity by donating money, sending in teddies or Calpol, and not connecting. We did the exact opposite. We've become parents to these kids. We can't walk away from them, or tell them that in a year there is no more money for them. To Russia With Love is a huge family, and we're all lucky to be a part of it, but there are huge responsibilities that come with this family.

As you read the stories of our children over the following pages, I hope you will see what their lives have been, and what they have and can become thanks to the work we do with the money you so generously give us. I hope you will continue to give generously, because our children need your help so badly.

Peter's Place

Peter's Place' is what our children call the flat in Bryansk that has become home, a point of contact and a place of refuge even for the ones who no longer live there, or have never lived there. You will read a lot about it in these next pages, so here is the story of how we got the flat, and what it means to us.

The flat is in a suburb of Byransk, on the tenth floor of a building where the lift never works. It looks like so many Russian flats. The area outside is practically rubble – no lawns, no flowers, no landscaping; piles of stones and earth, graffiti. Inside, the hall is bare concrete and badly-lit. The stairs are cold and run-down with peeling paint and rusty railings.

The flat itself is large, well laid-out, and cheery. It probably wouldn't be considered much here, but to our kids, it's a palace. And in fairness, it is a fine flat, designed and maintained with one idea in mind – to be a place where our children, the ones going on to college in Bryansk, can live while they study, and gradually find their feet in the outside world, watched over by us. Over the years, that flat has been home for so many of our children, and our home in Russia.

We sit around that table and we discuss everything under the sun. We've celebrated everything there, from weddings to funerals. It couldn't be a more emotional place. The last day I was there, the Irish ambassador, Eoin O'Leary, was with me, having tea with the boys. It is a fantastic place, and we have had fantastic successes come out of it.

The flat was bought by Peter Gannon. Peter was a friend of mine, and a great supporter of To Russia With Love, who died unexpectedly and way too soon, in July 2013.

Peter came into my life in a very low-key, unexpected way about ten years before he died, and consistently showed himself to be an exceptionally thoughtful young man with a heart of gold. Sadly this same heart had a weakness that none of us knew about, including himself.

He said he wanted to take children off the streets and decided to pick a couple of projects and take it from there. He built a school in Thailand, and he did some projects with us. I told him to pick whatever projects he wanted to do in Russia. He decided he wanted to buy a flat to make sure our children didn't end up on the streets, and he wanted a building project that he could be hands on involved in, because he was a builder and, more importantly, because he cared.

One of our baby orphanages, a terribly sweet place, needed new kitchens and toilets because it was very rundown at the time, so Peter went in with his clipboard and his attention to detail to see exactly what needed to be done, project-managed it all himself, paid the builders, did everything. Then he bought the much-used and talked-about flat in Bryansk, and redesigned it to his specifications, knocking down walls so the place was more open-plan.

He met some of our older boys, went on a few nights out with them, and got very involved with different people in our organisation. He also built a second playground in Hortolova designed by Dermot Hearne, a teacher in the prison system and the prisoners in Wheatfield prison. He was in Russia three times in all, and would have gone more often except for his fear of flying.

Peter died a year ago. He had a heart issue that he did not know about. He left behind many broken hearts and his two adored dogs, Ernie and Ozzie.

Peter was a remarkable young man. We should all be raising

Peter was a remarkable young man. We should all be raising our children to think of others, to try and do something, however small, that engages with the world and the lives of other, less fortunate people. Peter did that. He died too young, but he did a lot with his life before he left us, far more than most.

our children to think of others, to try and do something, however small, that engages with the world and the lives of other, less fortunate people. Peter did that. He died too young, but he did a lot with his life before he left us, far more than most.

I hope my own son does a fraction of the good Peter did.

So that is the story of Peter's Place, a flat that means everything to our children. It is their safe place, somewhere they know they can go when they really need to. Peter left it in a trust to To Russia With Love, so we will never lose it.

Choosing who gets to live in Peter's Place is very difficult, and I hate doing it. But we can't house them all, so either we house none, or we choose ones we know can survive and thrive there. The first condition is that every child there has to be going to college. It is a place to live while they finish their education. You can't put children in there who aren't well-behaved, because it's not supervised.

They get chosen carefully so we know there won't be drugs, drink or sex there. And of course we've gone in unexpectedly sometimes and found a girl running down the stairs in high heels, but that is very minor stuff, in fact, it's what young people should be doing, although we don't say that to them. In general, they are very good. Olga Stepanova, To Russia With Love programme director, runs the place like a Sergeant Major, and for all that she is so beautiful and kind, they are a little afraid of her and they toe the line.

There are officially seven beds, but we've often gone in to find five or six more kids who have spent the night because they don't have anywhere else. If we have any emergency cases or any kind of trauma among the older children, we take them in there. Post-army, that's where we take them, and nurse them back to the person they were before, because military service is a huge shock to their systems. Even though they are used to hardship, the army is very hard for them, because there are huge bullying problems, and our children have no one to say a word for them. They are the very bottom of the pecking order, and so they tend to come out after their year skinny, shocked and traumatised. It takes time and gentle minding to get them back on their feet again.

When Pasha, one of our most popular boys, was murdered the year after he left Hortolova, Peter's Place is where all our children gathered. Everybody was so upset. They had a photo of him on the table, with a candle burning in front of it through the night. They all grew up that night, as they made plans for how to get a grave, what he should wear to be buried in, how to conduct the service. All night, there was knocking on the door as the word spread, and by eight o'clock in the morning, there were about 50 young people there who had come from far and wide as the news spread. They knew that Peter's Place was where they would find us; it's our family home, except that in our family there are hundreds of children.

One of our boys, Andrei Danelkin, has a small photo of Peter stuck on his wall, surrounded by Russian icons. Andrei is deeply religious, and Peter is his inspiration, because of what he did for them. Andrei has had great difficulties in his life – his story appears over the page – and the idea of Peter keeps him going. These children don't have much to latch onto, there is so little kindness in their lives, that when they see a beam of kindness, it means everything to them, and they hold on to that. For Andrei, Peter is still that beam.

Here is a letter that Andrei wrote and sent to Peter's parents Gerry and Margaret Gannon shortly before before Peter's one-year anniversary.

Dear Margaret, Gerry, Sarah and Rita and everybody in my beloved Gannon family.

This is Andrei Danilkin writing. On July 6th we will commemorate one year after Peter's death. I want to say that he is still in our hearts and will be with us forever. I would like to say my words of sympathy to you all from all boys living in Peter's Place now and from all boys and girls you met when you were in Russia.

When I met you first, I wanted to say many words about the role that Peter had in my life. But all very very emotional, Margaret was crying and I didn't say what I wanted to say then. I would like to use this chance and say those words now. I am very happy that I knew Peter and that he became part of my life. He was a great young man. The fact that he bought a flat for all orphanage leavers and he didn't even say to you about that, says much about him.

The purchase of this flat supported lots of orphanage leavers for many years. If you take my personal story, as you know after the 2nd year in navy school I had an accident and was expelled from that school. I didn't have anywhere to live, was homeless. I did not receive any help from my relatives. The only option I saw was to return to Bryansk and to live at the train station with the understanding that I would never have money to rent or buy any accommodation.

I asked To Russia With Love for help. When I arrived to Bryansk by train, I was met by Olga at the train station and she brought me to Peter's Place. When I came there, I got a feeling of being welcomed, I felt love and care. Until that moment I didn't know about that flat. I was very happy to be there and after some time I was sure that with such support I will be able to get back to navy school as it was my dream. And I managed to do so thanks to Peter and all the support I got from TRWL. I would like to thank you for the present that you passed to me.

I also very much appreciate the keyrings with Peter's photos that you presented us. Also I have Peter's photo on the wall next to my bed. Every morning when I wake up the first thing that I see is Peter's photo and icons. And I have a feeling that Peter says to me every morning "Everything will be fine." And it gives me strength and support every day.

Even though Peter is not with us at the moment but I know one thing – his soul, his kindness, his love and care is with us and will always be with us. Peter was a very beautiful man. I often go to the church now and I always light a candle for Peter's memory. And also I lit a candle for all of Gannon family to stay well and healthy. Hope you will come to Russia some day in the future and we can go to the church together.

At the end of my letter I want to say – take care and God bless you.

My warmest regards

Andrei Danilkin

Peter died at 31, far too young, but in a very few years he made a huge impact on bettering the lives of so many young people. What he did leaves a lasting and worthwhile heritage behind. He realised the importance of providing a safe place for vulnerable young people. We are proud to have known and loved him and through Peter's Place his memory will live on in the hearts of many.

Rest in peace Peter - We will always love you.

❋

A still from 'Anya', Brown Bag Film's five minute, animated short which has had over 100,000 views online.

No. No. No. Yes.
By Damien O'Connor

Damien O'Connor is a director, writer, editor and producer who has been twice nominated for a prestigious Irish Film and Television Award. Classically trained as a 2D animator, Damien has worked as documentary producer and live broadcast director. He is the director of Anya, a five-minute animated short inspired by the work of To Russia With Love.

I f this were a film, my first encounter with Debbie Deegan would probably be in the comedy farce genre. I was in work one day, at Brown Bag Films, when Debbie, who I had never met or spoken to before, rang me out of the blue to ask if I would be interested in making a short advert to highlight the work that To Russia With Love do. I calmly explained that this was impossible, as animation is insanely time-consuming and expensive, and I just did not have the time. Truth is I also did not have the interest.

I suspect like many people, when I heard the words 'Russian orphans' I pictured grim VHS footage, a vision of hell, where filthy kids stare blankly from cots in abject misery. Very admirable that someone wanted to help these guys, but it was not for me. Of course all this went unsaid as Debbie continued to list reasons why I should help. For every reason given I had a 'no'. I had every variation of 'no.' I had more nos than a clown troupe. It was, I believed, a perfect storm of 'no,' but this woman I had never spoken to before, continued to speak. For every argument against she had a counter argument for. I was running out of reasons, so I fell back on the tried and tested method of hanging up.

I returned to my desk.

There was an email waiting for me.

It was from Debbie Deegan.

'So, when do we start?'

In hindsight it is exactly this brash, ballsy drive that enabled her to rebuild an orphanage in Russia, but I knew none of this at the time, what I did know is I found it amusing … if not a little unnerving.

But I was intrigued enough to go to the website.

And it was there that I began to read the children's own stories. These stories were not some objective observer recounting the horrors of their subjects; these were first person accounts from the children themselves. They were written in the raw, brutally honest language of children. All so chirpy and matter of fact as they trotted through the horrors of finding parents dead, seeing fathers murdered, being found by police as their mothers tried to sell them at markets... No flourishes, no manipulation, no delicate prose to embellish their pasts, just the excited gushing of children talking in the 'How I spent my summer holiday' language of primary school essays. These were not the voices of feral children, these were the voices of my children, of your children, of children everywhere. These were the voices of children in desperate need of help, care and love.

I replied to Debbie. I could not take on the job myself but I could assist her when it came to finding someone who could. Like a cat waiting to be let out, this was the crack in the door she needed. No sooner had I hit send, then my journey with the whirlwind force of nature that is Debbie Deegan began.

I read her biography, a stunning story of determination and heartache. I read up about the charity, I read the non-stop flow of emails arriving in from Debbie herself, a train-of-thought-monologue of ideas and plans for the ad. My offer to assist had clearly become an offer to do. Somewhere along the line, I had boarded the train. But what a train it was. I quickly jettisoned the idea of helping out, I would take on the job in full, but I knew there was no point in doing an advert. A short 30-second sting would help no one. It would go out into the chaotically busy freeway of information that is the internet and be immediately buried in the noise there. Before I had realised it myself, my refusal to help had turned into an offer to make a full film.

The plan was simple – we would make a full five-minute short film as a piece of entertainment. If people liked it, they could thank us by sending a donation to the charity. I looked on it as a film equivalent of a Christmas charity single or a charity calendar.

People would be more likely to share a film with friends and family, which would help increase awareness of the charity.

All nice and easy … with one major glaring exception – I would now have to make it.

The traditional route to making a short film is to have an amazing idea, hone it into a brilliant script, send the script out for funding, get money, begin production. It can take years to go from script to screen. I didn't even have a script never mind an idea, but I did have one thing – the voices of the children themselves.

I went back to the children's stories and began to jot down ideas. I came up with a framing device of a children's bedtime story. A 'once upon a time fairy-tale' about a little lost girl in the woods who finds an orphanage. We see the girl explore her world – To Russia With Love and the amazing staff at the orphanage help her grow – she grows into a young woman, she leaves and gets her own home. And the payoff, the woman telling the bedtime story to her own child is the now fully-grown little girl we saw at the start.

I sent it to Debbie, she replied in the positive. I drew up story-boards and recorded temporary narration. I began to look into the best and cheapest way to make the film. And then Debbie suggested I come to Russia to meet the children myself.

I leapt at the chance and it is a testament to Debbie's enthusiasm that she could turn a man who wanted nothing to do with Russian orphans into a man itching to go to a Russian orphanage in the space of a few weeks.

The first day at the orphanage was surreal. It was last bell, a traditional family day in Russia where they celebrate the kids leaving school. The kids were dressed in black tie; even four-year-olds were wearing dickey-bows, the girls wore mini ball gowns with huge flower wreaths in their hair. As far removed as you can get from the grainy images of horror I grew up with on the news, but no less heart-breaking. Given the juxtaposition between a day of bright happy celebration and the huge glaring absence of family members, the colourful costumes felt like a mortuary painted in bright primary colours.

The kids put on an elaborate show, and with every song, every dance routine, every faltered poem the heartache grew. Eventually we all moved outside. The kids had written their wishes for the future on white balloons. As they released them, the balloons soared up and the kids and adults clapped and cheered. Then one balloon began a sideways descent, it slowly fell back to earth, bounced across the potholed pavement and came to rest against behind a shabby stone wall. There was a brief flurry of discussion among the kids, should they check the balloon, see whose wish would not come to fruition. A decision was made – the kids all ran back inside and the balloon was left anonymous.

That evening we went to a graduation dinner. The restaurant-come-dance-floor was packed with families. Our own table, with 20 children to five adults, was clearly different. The kids stood and touchingly, used a little microphone to give speeches. All praised Debbie and the work of TRWL.

One girl with excellent English gave a rousing speech about how her life had transformed, but she was heartbroken to leave the orphanage and venture out on her own. All day she had seemed distracted and anxious. After the speech, she wept on and off. By 11pm the bus had arrived to bring the kids home to the orphanage. As she made her way on to the bus, this girl became hysterical. She climbed back off and began to show me photos on her mobile phone.

They were pictures of a baby in the arms of an unseen male.

Between sobs she was repeating a question in Russian. She was eventually helped back on the bus. I later asked what it had all been about. Apparently she had wandered into the orphanage one day and toddled up to an orphanage worker. She calmly explained her dad had dropped her off and told her to find an adult. He needed to go away for two weeks to play music in bars.

That was seven years ago.

He has never returned.

In the most cruel twist of all, he writes to her annually to tell her he is on his way back to collect her. She eventually came to believe that if he was ever going to arrive back, it would be to see her celebrate Last Bell. As the day drew to an end it became obvious he was not coming. The photos on her phone were her, the unseen male her dad. Her question, a simple 'why?'

Day two. The kids were thankfully out of costume and back in kid's clothes. The entire atmosphere was different; the place was relaxed, the kids mucked about on bikes, shouts and laughs mingled with bird song. The kids were cheerfully curious, 'why was I there, taking photos of seemingly random objects?' Olga, one of the nicest, most caring humans I have ever met translated; I was making a film about them. The kids laughed, 'why would anyone watch a film about them?'

By the afternoon, myself and a small group of the kids had become buddies. I filmed them acting out scenes from my story-boards – they ran around screaming with joy – a welcome break from their monotony of day-to-day orphanage life (you can see the footage on the end titles of the film).

This was also the day I met Sasha. We had spent the afternoon filming and it had become clear that if anyone embodied the fictional character of Anya, it was her. At the start she was shy and faltering, by the end she was clearly the lead actress. During a break from filming, a man arrived and began to hand out lollipops, all the kids queued patiently, running off when the lollipop was handed over. Little Sasha got hers and ran to me, she insisted I take it. I refused, but she was adamant to the point of getting upset. As I took the lollipop she reached over and put her hand around my thumb and gave it a tiny little squeeze before running off to join her mates. I had just experienced the world's smallest hug.

When I got back to Dublin, it was apparent that the film in its current form would not work. It was an adult's interpretation of what it meant to be a child in an orphanage. The fairy-tale narration was way off, making it twee and romantic. It was also the world's worst 'guess what I did when I was an orphan?' bedtime story.

The film had no trace of hope. In order to work, the film needed to be bigger and grander. We dismissed the idea of cheap and cheerful and instead put out an appeal for volunteers among the people I work with. The response was immediate, name after name lined up to offer to help. I wrote to a studio we know in Singapore, I relayed my trip to them, begged for assistance. They replied they would be happy to offer the studio services for free. The film we wanted to make was now looking like a distinct possibility.

I went back to the script, threw out the narration and reworked the opening and ending. Little Sasha became my Anya. I fortunately never heard Sasha's back story, just as we never hear Anya's – the fact that they are in an orphanage is enough to know it must be grim. Whilst meeting the kids improved the film a thousand times over, it also increased the pressure to get it right. All in all, it took about six weeks of editing and work to get the script to a version we felt did the kids justice. I pitched the new version to Debbie, explaining that I had removed all narration outlining the work TRWL do. She calmly watched both versions and then agreed the no-narration version worked better. An amazing leap of faith from a client.

That was March 2013.

Thirteen months later I was on my way back to the orphanage to premiere the film for the kids. On the plane over it dawned on me that I was about to assemble a group of orphans in an orphanage to screen a poignant film about being an orphan. What was I thinking? The film's producer, the ever-patient and optimistic Edel Byrne, admitted she had similar concerns. Even Debbie herself had begun to air doubts; did we 'really' have to screen the last shot? Would it upset the kids? We even considered contacting the studio in Dublin to ask them to send over a version with some of the more poignant shots removed.

As a filmmaker, this kind of thing would normally be hell on earth, but Debbie's concerns for the children over-rides anything else. If there were the slightest chance they could be upset, the film would be changed. When we arrived we discussed our concerns with the orphanage workers and we screened the film for them (adorably, they had painted the main hall in the orphanage and put in curtains for the premiere, because they wanted the kids to know it was a big event). They decision amongst the workers was unanimous – the kids should see it in its full form.

As the hours ticked towards the screening, the atmosphere once again changed as the kids donned dickie bows and ball gowns. A news crew arrived with the Governor of Bryansk. The kids lined up in amazing traditional Russian outfits. The formality of the occasion had the children on edge, so Edel and I spent a large part of the morning messing about with them to get them to loosen up. After another perfectly performed concert from the kids, the film began. I sat next to Sasha. I was terrified. First screenings are rarely pleasant but here I was, an adult from Dublin, about to tell a group of orphans what I thought their lives were like. As the film played I searched Sasha's face for any trace of upset. There was none, just the face of a child transfixed by a cartoon. She could recognise herself, her buddies, the locations, the sounds ... and they thought it was a hoot. As the lights came up I looked over to the adult's side of the room, tears were being wiped away. I looked back at the kids surrounding me, smiles all around.

The day after the premiere, I was brought to a different orphanage. This one was for babies. Cot after cot of tiny little bundles, all lying quietly. In one cot, two little kids sat side by side. One blond, one dark. They had spent their three short years of life together in the same cot. The connection they had was palpable. Then we heard the dark-haired boy had been fostered. He was due to be taken away in a week. The blond-haired boy had no idea what awaited. He just stared out the bars of his cot, curious about the rabble of adults before him. Any elation about the premiere vanished. His screams as he lost the only friend he had ever known would drown out any memory of applause. And here it was, the grainy VHS images I had grown up with right in front of my eyes. But I no longer wanted to shy away, I wanted to embrace him and make him feel better.

That trip, to the baby orphanage, made the film feel a little bit like holding a tiny bin lid against an impending tidal wave of misery. Yes the response has been amazing, but for every nomination, festival and kind comment, I still see an abandoned little boy in a cot. These children need so much more than a short film. They need a sense of self-worth, a sense of belonging, a sense of being loved.

And yet, a week after I returned to Dublin I was sent a video. It was the kids in the orphanage watching a DVD of the film. Apparently they have it on a loop in their playroom. They watch it and point out their cartoon images to each other. Little Sasha has gone from following the group to leading the group. She feels, justifiably, that she is a movie star. If the kids were now to ask me why anyone would watch a film about their lives, I could answer that over 100,000 people have.

If the film lets them know that people around the world care about them, then it has done its job. This is what To Russia with Love spends every day working towards – the chance to make children feel loved, the chance to change lives. But the thing is, To Russia With Love doesn't just change the lives of the children in their care, they change the lives of everyone they bring with them. I am reluctant to even write that as it brings the emphasis to my story, and this should not be a story about me, or even the charity, it should be a story about the thousands upon thousands of abandoned and orphaned children in the Russian Federation.

In Russia, the success of Anya has been due to the efforts of Andrei Malakhov, Oksana Fedorova, Chulpan Khamatova, Anna Yablokova and Gerry McCarthy who have spread the word and championed the film and To Russia With Love with tremendous enthusiasm and energy.

Spending a few hours in Hortolova orphanage can give you a sense that the problem is solved. For every balloon that soared, there are thousands more lying abandoned behind shabby stone walls.

82 people across five countries spent 15 months making Anya. It has over 100,000 views online, has been nominated for two awards and has been screened at five festivals (and counting).

✳

"For every balloon that soared, there are thousands more lying abandoned behind shabby stone walls."

75

A transformative journey
Mary Kennedy

Mary Kennedy is a broadcaster and RTE Nationwide presenter

I visited Hortolova with Debbie nearly three years ago, and the reason I went is because I had done a few things for Debbie here in Ireland – fundraising, hosting events – and I felt that by going and seeing the projects, I would be better able to understand, and be of more help. In fact, so impressed was I by what I saw in Russia that we ended up doing a piece for Nationwide while I was there.

What really made an impression on me was the holistic way these children were cared for, their well-being. This comes from the fact that they are well educated, well fed, and loved, and starts with the bright and cheerful environment they lived in.

Arriving at Hortolova, it is the colour of the buildings that really stands out. Debbie showed the children palettes and asked them to choose the colours they would like for the new living quarters she then set about providing. Where once everything was grey or beige, there is now a lot of pink and lilac and bright blue.

But it is not just bricks and mortar and a coat of paint. It is a difference in attitude that sees the emotional and educational

Mary Kennedy during her trip to Hortolova

development of the children as central. The single word 'love' covers it. It was absent. Now it is everywhere.

Hortolova was far more than I thought it would be. More impressive, more touching, more colourful, more varied. I loved the downtime with the young girls doing their embroidery and sewing. The way there are only four to a bedroom. The poetry and songs. The traditional costumes in which they danced. The confidence with which one girl told me she wanted to be a translator when she grew up.

Thankfully for these children, Debbie Deegan is a woman with a huge heart, energy and passion. Not for her the backward glance. She set about changing the circumstances of the children she found in Hortolova, practically and emotionally. The thing she felt they were lacking most was love, and now they have it in spades!

I remember the first day I arrived, all the children came out to greet Debbie and absolutely smothered her with hugs and kisses. One little boy stood back from the rest. He was paler than the other children, thinner, he had a sore on his mouth, matted hair, and was clearly not part of the group. I felt so sorry for him. The difference between him and the rest of the children was very marked – physically, but also psychologically – and I learned that he had just arrived at Hortolova.

He was new to life there, and so did not yet understand what this affection was. He just didn't know how to be happy. I still remember him so well. The other children were secure, they had their bright houses in the orphanage compound, the playground, many brightly coloured toys – their lives were full of yellows, reds, purples, pinks – whereas his still seemed so grey.

We also visited a baby centre on that trip that To Russia With

Love helps. These are little ones with mental and physical disabilities, whose parents couldn't or wouldn't have anything to do with them, and who were abandoned at birth. It is heartbreaking to lift a tiny scrap from her cot who weighs about two kilos and is seven months old.

Or to hold a baby with obvious foetal alcohol syndrome because his mother drank right through pregnancy. Or to cradle a baby born with AIDS because her mother is a junkie. And yet, it is uplifting to witness the loving and caring environment that these little babies inhabit. Because that too was a bright, warm, loving place, with mobiles and music carousels over the cots, and those babies were like puppies in the way they responded to being held and hugged.

What is heartbreaking is not the day-to-day life of these children that Debbie and her team have taken under their wings, it is the back-stories. These are not orphans the way we understand the word, instead they are victims of neglect, or alcoholism, or a second marriage in which the new partner won't take on another man's kids. They are victims of a system that doesn't put them or their emotional needs first.

The children in Hortolova feel this is the first time anyone has cared for them, and they are right. They are in a nurturing, stimulating environment. This is a home, in a way their original homes never were – they were toxic, dangerous places, and the children's lives were headed down a slippery slope. Then they were taken into care, and, quite frankly, they won the lottery.

These are the very, very lucky ones who have ended up under Debbie and her Russian and Irish colleagues wings. The shame of it is that there are so many, many more who haven't and can't.

I think love is what keeps Debbie doing this. She had her own children, then she made this promise, and she kept it, because she just couldn't turn her back. There are other people who see things like this, who feel like she did, but they don't do anything about it. Debbie is a very driven woman – even the way she has made a success of the shop here shows that; one of its greatest qualities is the awareness it raises of To Russia With Love, not just the money. Also, Debbie has a conscience. That might be an old-fashioned word, but it is the right one.

She ended up in this place, she saw the broken windows, smelled the stench in the corridors, saw the broken waifs, and she realised, 'its up to me to do something about it, or not. If I don't, no one else will.' That sense of responsibility, of the right thing to do, drives her. She is somebody who has that conscience, that sense of justice. I think what irritates her is that she can only do it on this scale, which is a big scale, but not big enough for her.

What made the deepest impression on me is the way the children respond to Debbie. She is very charismatic and they adore her. They all want to touch her, hug her, be held by her. She is their mother. She gives them the love they need, and she gets it back. Once you see that, you feel that they are in safe hands, and their future is in safe hands. Debbie will never turn her back on them. That's the way she is.

I know they say charity begins at home, but these orphans of Debbie's are just children. They didn't ask to be born into these difficult circumstances, and they need all the help they can get. Because Debbie does it, we don't have to; all we have to do is help her to help them. Debbie is a doer, and because of that, we get to be helpers.

As Mother Teresa said, don't think about numbers, just help

one person at a time. If you can change one person's life, it has been worth it. To Russia With Love has changed many children's lives, and each one of those children will go on to bring and be further change in the lives of those around them.

The hook well set
Joanna Fortune

Joanna Fortune is a clinical Psychotherapist and Child Attachment Specialist. She runs her Solamh Parent Child Relationship Clinic in Dublin where she works with children, adolescents and parents. Joanna has previously worked in the NGO sector for 12 years including almost 4 years as CEO of To Russia With Love. Joanna's clinical specialty is repairing attachment wounds in children.

My first experience of a meeting in Russia was with the staff of Hortolova Orphanage where we were discussing To Russia With Love's plan to bring all of the children to the seaside for our anniversary. It had been a great fundraising year and we were delighted to be in a position to celebrate with the children. I met with the staff to run through the itinerary expecting that they would be as excited as we were about the trip. Not so! They spent 1 hour 15 minutes outlining to me (via interpreters so you can imagine how long this went on) the myriad of ways that this trip we were proposing was a terrible idea and how impossible it would make their jobs.

After and hour and a quarter I caved and said "OK we won't do it if this is impossible," and was met with shock as they exclaimed, "of course we will do it, it will happen!" And so I learned this is how business got done in Russia, you present an idea, get told countless problems with your "terrible" idea only to have everyone pull together and ensure it gets done beautifully, professionally, lovingly done each time.

People often wonder how Debbie Deegan, a self-proclaimed housewife from Clontarf, (though her true CV is far more encompassing than this title elucidates,) has managed to do business in Russia for so long and with such amazing results. Having watched her do it firsthand I can only say that it is because Debbie has a unique way of bringing people with her, no matter who they are and no matter what the project is.

The hook is the children, they were and still are the hook for her, and for anyone who has ever been to Hortolova – and there is no stronger hook than 100 parentless children. I always said that working with To Russia With Love and Debbie Deegan in particular was never a job, it was a lifestyle choice, and I stand by that.

Debbie and I are very different people and anyone who knows us is initially quite perplexed as to how we managed to work so well together in spite of our differences but I think we worked so well together because of our differences! Don't get me wrong, there were days when our differences would cause a fall out and it was no strange sight to find me sitting with my hands over my ears humming "la, la, la," pretending not to hear whatever scheme Debbie was suggesting, but ultimately we would argue, talk and work it out and get the job done because there were hundreds of children and young people depending on us to do so and that pressure never eases up and never ceases to motivate.

I consider Debbie Deegan to be a true friend and will forever admire and appreciate what she has done for the lives of children in Russia's once forgotten orphanages.

Outside of my role in To Russia With Love I am a psychotherapist and attachment specialist, working with children, adolescents and their parents. I work daily repairing early attachment wounds with adopted and cared for children, and would like to pay particular tribute to the astounding work of To Russia With Love in attending to the attachment needs of children growing up without parents.

"Over time, with lots of love, support, patience and understanding, these scared and abandoned, broken little children are gradually put back together and begin to smile and laugh."

The social brain is 50% developed by the age of one year old and 90% developed by the age of three years old, with social and environmental factors making the difference. At this young age, trust is the first developmental milestone for children. When babies and small children learn to trust during this period, their developing brains become wired to trust throughout life.

Trust develops when a baby can count on their needs being met by emotionally available caregivers. Responsive, attuned caregiving gives a baby's brain the message that the world is a safe place and that people can be depended upon. Research shows that children whose cries are consistently met in the first year cry less and sleep better. Children whose cries prompt appropriate responses tend to develop into independent, confident and self-regulating children.

This is how vitally important these early years are to developing  children, and not one child under To Russia With Love's care has had these essential early developmental needs met when they arrive on a bus, alone, scared with everything they own in the world contained in the one shabby suitcase they grasp tightly in their tiny hands.

I have seen these scared little faces suspiciously eyeing up the kind faces of the To Russia With Love staff who greet them, take them by the hand to show them around, gift them a welcome pack with their own tooth brush, hair brush, teddy and pyjamas and stay with them when they join the other children in the designated playroom for a welcome party.

These scared little faces have softened by the time their photo goes onto the "our family" picture chart and their birthdays are added to the calendar, and over time, with lots of love, support, patience and understanding, these scared and abandoned, broken little children are gradually put back together and begin to smile and laugh.

Anytime I'm asked how To Russia With Love achieves what it does, I have to say that I cannot name any one specific big thing that

To Russia With Love does but that it is the countless little things that are done quietly, unassumingly and daily that make the difference and how do you measure the outcome of that? Well you look at the broken and traumatised little girl who arrived, having witnessed her father murder her mother's lover and provided the witness statement that saw him sent to prison for 10 years now completing training as a doctor.

You look at the beautiful successful girl who arrived sad and alone after her mother abandoned her to the care of the state when her new husband wouldn't have another man's child in his home as she graduates as an accountant. Or the sad and silent little boy who didn't speak to anyone and never made eye contact, now working as a lawyer, married with his own child.

You look at that first group of children Debbie Deegan met all those years ago, promising that she would come back to hug and kiss them, now independent adults with lives, careers and families of their own...a generation for whom the cycle of addiction, poverty and child abandonment is broken, a generation of hundreds of healed and mended spirits.

On my darkest, most frustrated days working in orphanages in the lonely forests of Russia, I would take out two pictures and feel motivated all over again. They were done by a little girl (four years old) who arrived with her two brave older brothers (six and eight years old), having lived on the streets for weeks.

One of her brothers had walked into the department of education and asked that the three of them be put in an orphanage as he could no longer take care of them all on his own. His sister drew an empty black house.

Many months later she drew another house, colourful, with hearts for windows and flowers growing alongside it and a blue sky.

The work and life mission of To Russia With Love is to teach children how to love and be loved again and it was a great privilege and honour to be a small part of that journey. We all got a lot more from those children than we ever could give them

I remember the heady days where a developer might hand you a €10,000 cheque standing at a bar at a fundraiser. I even remember Caprice's thong and Jordan's bra fetching an eye-watering €10,000 each at auction, and the lengths we could make that money stretch was impressive. But those days are gone and now it is really hard to keep funding things like welcome packs for new arrivals or cooking classes so even small children can start to learn how to take care of themselves.

To Russia With Love is about the small things with big impact but without money those small things are getting smaller, and less and less children are feeling the reach of the great work, with staff cut back to a bare minimum. Every euro in a donation bucket or €4 text sent is making a life-changing impact in the lives of these children, and more and more donations like this are badly needed right now because sadly children still arrive on those buses with their little broken worlds held in those shabby suitcases.

To Russia With Love has been a success story based on the effort of the hard working committed staff on the ground who love and care for these children. This is not science, nor is it complicated, it is simple and basic and consistent and unwavering and that is why it works. But without funding even simple and basic becomes inconsistent and wavering.

This work is too important to stop now, please give what you can to support this life-changing work because small changes really do make big differences in the lives of children.

✳

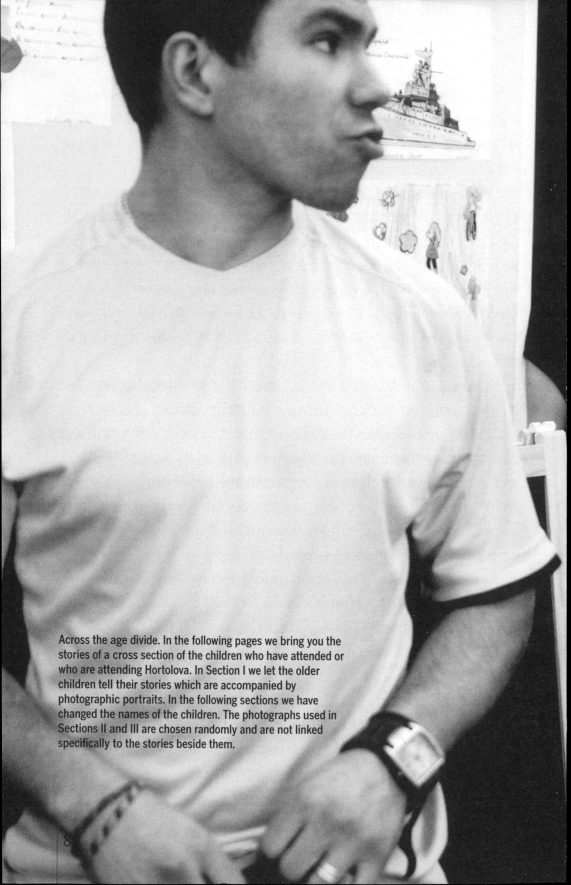

Across the age divide. In the following pages we bring you the
stories of a cross section of the children who have attended or
who are attending Hortolova. In Section I we let the older
children tell their stories which are accompanied by
photographic portraits. In the following sections we have
changed the names of the children. The photographs used in
Sections II and III are chosen randomly and are not linked
specifically to the stories beside them.

The Children's Stories Part 1

The young men and women who are now 26 and 27 years old are our most successful children so far. This was the first generation that fully benefited from the intervention of To Russia With Love. They were nine or 10 when we first arrived into Hortolova, and so they have had the full benefit of many years with us – and our wealthiest years. In those days, we could run a host of programmes to encourage their independence, creativity, socialisation and education; all of which had a huge impact on their psychological and intellectual development.

These kids have been our great success stories. We have seen then embark on life, and make a go of it. They have jobs, careers, skills, families; more importantly, they have a sense of themselves, and of optimism for the future. Their lives are still very hard –

Russia is a hard country, harder again for orphans in a society where so much works and happens through family connections and strings pulled – but we believe these young people will continue to make a go of it.

They are like family to each other, and to us. They have created bonds and a strong network of support that not one of them has through birth. Their birth families failed them and rejected them, but they have created new families, with us and with each other.

And we still support them as we can. Mainly through our friendship and love, rather than financially, because there is no money to spare in these difficult times, and every penny needs to go towards helping the younger children, still in Hortolova orphanage, who will never have the quality of life of our older boys and girls unless we can replicate the care given to that first generation.

It isn't easy. There is far less money now than there was in the heyday of the Irish boom, when To Russia With Love could raise tens of thousands of euros in one night. We have had to cut some programmes, scale back others, until we are operating at a very minimal level.

This is devastating for us because we know how much the extra programmes, the visits to the ice rink, a football club or a shopping centre contributed to the success of our older generation. We know that every one of those programmes had an effect on their development, their confidence and their abilities. Those outings and experiences weren't just fun, they also taught them vital skills, encouraged their ambition and abilities, and rounded out their education, equipping them for the world outside their forest clearing – a scary place for a child who has never bought anything in a shop for themselves, has never got a bus or a train, or found their own way to an unknown destination.

Orphans don't just miss out on the love of a family and the guidance of people who care about showing them the way to be. They are infantilised by a system that makes all their decisions for them. The daily outings and interactions, no matter how small and unimportant, that family children experience from the youngest age – orphan children do not experience this. As a result, adjustment to the freedom and indifference and pace of the outside world is very difficult. Many of them never make the transition. Ours did, because we built them up to it and taught them little by little how to manage.

Because we have trimmed our programmes in line with slashed budgets, we can no longer do everything that we once did. Knowing how much those programmes meant to our older children makes us very afraid for the younger ones, but determined to keep fighting and trying, for their sakes.

I have let these children them tell their own stories, because they are well able to do that. The extraordinary eloquence and emotional maturity of these kids – all the more amazing when you consider what they have been through – is compelling. Some had childhoods that were brutal, neglected and savage. The lucky ones have been institutionalised from the youngest age, sometimes from as little as a few months or a year old. And yet they can look at their lives, the things that have happened to them, and describe them so beautifully.

Until we came along, no one taught them how to express themselves. Now they do so with maturity, confidence and in a way that makes it impossible not to listen.

Here are their stories.

✳

Andrei Danilkin (26).
Student at the Naval Academy in Northern Russia

Andrei was put into an orphanage when he was six, after his mother killed his father, and was herself sent to jail. Andrei came to Hortolova when he was 10. He was a silent but wonderful child, kind, hard-working, determined. He has had many problems to face but has so far overcome them all with steady determination.

"I was born in Bryansk city. As far as I know, our family was quite a good family at the time I was born, but then Perestroika came, the movement for reformation from within the Communist party, and later the Soviet Union collapsed. That was a good thing in the eyes of the world, but in Russia it meant hard times for many people who lost their jobs and the way they were used to living. I don't remember what my father's job was before Perestroika, but I do know that he didn't work very much afterwards, and he, like so many others, had a hard time adjusting to the new economy. My family became dysfunctional. Our home stopped being a good one, and my parents started to drink heavily. As a child, I began to witness more and more drinking sessions.

Whatever they earned, they wasted on alcohol. Whatever child benefit they got, that went on alcohol too.

I was the only child, thanks be to God. I would hate to think of another child, a brother or sister, living the way I did then. By the time I was four or five, I knew to look through my neighbours' garbage, for food or something I could sell. I looked through the bins on the streets and outside shops. If I found a piece of bread, I

Andrei Danilkin: "I still have photos of myself in front of College Green, at the zoo, on days out. I stayed with Caroline Mahon and her kind family, but I was wild, I wasn't very sociable."

was happy. I did this to survive, often staying out for entire days and even nights. I knew there wouldn't be anything for me at home, so often I didn't bother going back there.

One day something happened. It did not seem like good luck at the time, it seemed terrible, but later I began to believe that it was, after all, luck. I was six years old that day, at school, in first class, and I was told to go home quick, because something had happened there. When I reached home, I saw a festive table was laid out. My parents were celebrating something, but they were short of alcohol. They had drunk everything they had, and they needed more. There was an argument over how they would find the money, and who would go and buy the vodka. They couldn't think of any way to get the money they needed, and they both became very angry, very aggressive, psychotic almost.

I was sitting beside the fireplace, and because I was trying to stop them shouting at each other, I was making noise. It was too much noise for my mum, who got irritated by me, and started to shout and hit me. My dad tried to defend me, which made her even angrier, so they started to fight each other, punching and slapping. Then my mum took a knife and stabbed my dad. I was small, I didn't realise then what had happened. I was also so used to all the fights they had, that I didn't realise this one was more serious.

But I was scared, so I ran away. Much later, in the middle of the night I returned home. My mum was asleep. My dad was lying on the floor. He asked me to give him a bucket to use as a toilet. I remember he was shivering. I thought he had a temperature or he was cold, so I went to try and get a blanket from under my sleeping mother, but I couldn't move her. Instead I gave him my blanket, and I lay on the floor beside him and fell asleep. In the morning, I got up and went to school. I was used to getting myself to school because I often didn't see my parents in the morning, so I still didn't realise how bad the situation was. That afternoon, I came home from school and I saw my father covered with a white sheet, many neighbours and family standing around, and everyone crying. Only then did I realise what had happened. My dad was dead, killed by my mother. I couldn't stay there, so I ran away again, and stayed away for a couple of days, wandering the streets,

"I have been very persistent, more so than I ever thought I could be, because I don't want to fail and lose the trust that Debbie has put in me. More than anything, I want to see her face at my graduation."

trying to keep warm and feed myself any way I could. The police found me eventually, and they took me to a shelter house.

I never saw my mum again. I have no good memories of her. The only thing I really remember is the green coat she wore. At the shelter house, they offered to bring me to prison to see my mum, or to court when she had a hearing, but I refused. I can't explain why, maybe I was too frightened? I hadn't seen her since she killed my dad. I don't know exactly what it was, but I knew I didn't want to see her at that time.

She was sent to jail for seven years, for murder. In all that time, she wrote me just one letter, in which she promised to come back and that we would start all over again, together. That she would be a mother to me and care for me. I was small, and desperate, so I believed her and spent a long time hoping and waiting for that to happen, this time of love and care that she wrote about. It was all I wanted in the world. But it never did happen. When eventually she was released, she came home, and started to drink again. She never sent for me, or came to see me. Her promise to take care of me never came to anything. I don't blame her. I still love her, in my own way.

After the shelter house I was sent to an orphanage for young children. It was the same orphanage where Zina was, before Debbie adopted her. I had to repeat my first year at school, because I couldn't cope with studying. I was in shock and I couldn't concentrate on my work after everything that had happened. But that was a good orphanage. They gave us good food, good clothes, the carers were kind to us.

I remember a trip to Ireland around this time, I think it was the same trip Zina went on, when she stayed with Debbie for the first time. I still have photos of myself in front of College Green, at the zoo, on days out. I stayed with Caroline Mahon and her kind family, but I was wild, I wasn't very sociable. In fact, I was frightened because I had never known a family so loving and caring as the Mahons, and it scared me. Maybe because once everything was so good in my family, but then it stopped and became so bad? Maybe I was afraid this would happen again? I don't know, but I couldn't trust, I wasn't easy with anything good and nice. To see a family, not my family, together, happy, loving, made me scared. I never went to Ireland again.

When I grew too big for that orphanage, I was sent to Hortolova, along with the rest of my class, who had also been Zina's classmates.

Hortolova in those days didn't look even close to what it looks like today. It was a very bad place to go to then, a very difficult place to live. There were no showers and we were usually dirty. We always had head lice, we wore worn out old shoes that had been handed down to us from older boys who had already worn them for three or four years. The shoes had holes, broken soles, no laces. I remember days when we didn't even have socks and it was cold and raining outside. I remember I got rubber boots somehow, but it wasn't a big joy to wear them with bare feet, so I took my old t-shirts and cut them up and made socks out of them.

The older boys did just what they liked, and no one interfered or tried to stop them. They were very aggressive with us younger ones. They stole from us, if we ever had anything to steal, and from each other. If they wanted a cigarette, they would stop a younger boy and demand one, even though we younger boys never had cigarettes, because where would we get them? We had no money, nothing. When we didn't give them what they wanted, we would be punched.

I was there in Hortolova, living like that, for maybe three years before Debbie came. Maybe it was less, maybe the days just seemed longer under such conditions? Then Debbie came, a ray of light, of sunshine, in that dark forest.

I clearly remember her first appearance. After so many years, when I look back and think about what happened that day, the way our lives began to change, I can't stop admiring her. On her first visit, somebody stole her passport and her wallet. Some older boys managed to find the thief and get them back, but I thought she would never come back, that this would be her first and last visit. A Russian person would not have come back. But she did, she started to help us in every way.

Things began to change very fast after Debbie came. The environment – she started to renovate and rebuild – was first, but psychologically it took a while for us children to understand that things could be different for us. If you adopt a street dog and take it home, that dog cannot show trust when it has been neglected and humans have been horrible to it for such a long time. It takes time. That was the same with us.

Until Debbie came, I didn't really care much what would happen to me. I didn't think of myself as anything. I saw how our leavers ended up – alcoholics, without jobs, in prison – and so I knew exactly what my destiny would be. Did you ever experience drowning, and someone came unexpectedly to help you? This is exactly like what happened; in my mind I compare Debbie's arrival with a hand coming down from the sky, reaching out and lifting us up.

If it had not been for Debbie, every one of us would have drowned in the shit we lived in.

Through Debbie and the Irish who came with her, we started to get help in every way – with our schooling, health, general education, even sport; any sport we wanted to do, we could. Any subjects we wanted to learn, we were encouraged. We had chances like never before, and gradually, we began to realise that we could want something better, that we could think about our lives and wish for things, and we might achieve these things. We saw there was somebody who cared for us, who wanted us to be good, to be our best, and because of that, because of the belief of these Irish people, we didn't want to fail.

Thanks to Debbie's belief and love, and the programme of extra grinds and extra activities, I managed to get into the naval academy. Before Debbie came, no one from Hortolova went to third level education. The best careers we could hope for were maybe plumber, bricklayer or tractor driver – all the shitty professions that family children don't want to do. Most of our leavers didn't even do those jobs for very long; quickly they started to drink and then they disappeared, into prison or into the forest, or dead.

Before Debbie, everyone would have laughed if I had said I even thought about being a military man. It would have been too ridiculous, like saying I wanted to fly. But after Debbie arrived, I knew that I could do it. So I started on my own at first, I went to military offices to collect the necessary papers, I began to prepare for the entrance exams. Then a new director came to the orphanage, who had connections in the military world, and he helped me greatly. My last year in school was very intensive. I had so many gaps to fill in, to bring my education up to the level needed, that I had to study constantly.

It was very hard; constant work, constant preparation. I thought about letting go of the idea, but I never did. The thing that kept me going was, I knew this was worth doing. By then I had begun to see other orphanage leavers going into third level education, so I knew I could do it, and I wanted to. We were the first group from Hortolova to ever achieve anything, and I knew very well that this was my chance to make something from my life.

I did the entrance exams, and I passed them. I was enrolled. That was such a proud moment for me. After the terrible things that happened to me, finally I had the chance to become better.

The military college is in the north west of Russia, on the other side of Latvia, very far away. I wasn't scared to go that far, I was too excited. And once I got there, it was easy for me to adapt. Military college was another kind of institution, and I was already institutionalised. I didn't know anything about the kind of soft family life the other cadets came from, with apple pies and star charts, so I was much more able for it than they were. Also, I was very sporty and very disciplined, and that's exactly the kind of cadet the college wanted. I'm not that fit now, but at that time, I was extremely fit; all the physical exercise was easy enough.

The course was five years in total, and when I was in my third year in college, another terrible thing happened. I had a day off, a bank holiday. I went to the park with friends. We weren't drinking, just talking, messing. At about midnight we were on our way back to the academy, by foot. We had a road to cross, at a pedestrian crossing. Two of my friends were a few steps in front of me, two were behind, and two of us were walking side by side. We were hit by a car, run over. The car didn't stop and I never found out who was driving. My friend was much luckier than me, he had a few bones broken, but I wasn't lucky. I was left with a very severe brain injury.

There was a large bleed in my brain, and it clotted. The pressure on the brain was so great that the doctors cut a large piece of my skull away and drained the blood. They then put a metal plate in my head to patch it up, which is still there. It felt very strange at first, but now I am used to it.

I was in the intensive care unit, unconscious, for a few weeks, and then it was six more months before anyone in To Russia With Love was told what had happened, because the academy was so far away. After being unconscious for so long, I was confused for a time. I didn't really realise myself what had happened, and I couldn't think of telling anyone. My constant worry was – would they keep me in the academy or not? Mine was a very serious injury, and you have to be perfectly fit to be a military man or in the navy. I asked the doctors, who said, you will have very intensive rehabilitation period. If you follow the advice and do what you are told, you will be completely fine, but that's all we can do; it's up to your officers in the academy whether they keep you or not.

My head of the department was a good guy, he liked me, he could see I worked hard and was determined to do well, and so he wanted to take me back.

Over a period of two years I had enormous difficulties maintaining my place within the Academy – but now I am returning in September and I am looking forward to resuming my studies and my life within the institution.

I have to go back to the beginning of the third year, which means I still have three more years to complete. But it's the only way they will accept me back, and so I will take it – and I am very grateful for the opportunity to do so.

Because of that, I need to be incredibly fit, fitter than the 20-year-olds, more disciplined, more hard working, more determined than any of them. This is my last chance to achieve what I want with my life.

I have been very persistent, more so than I ever thought I could be, because I don't want to fail and lose the trust that Debbie has put in me. More than anything, I want to see her face at my graduation, her pride when she sees that I have succeeded, with the help she gave me. Apart from the lessons, the trips, the sports, the Irish and all To Russia With Love staff have given me belief in myself. Through them, I learned how to trust people, to ask for help and let people give it to me. God knows where I would be without Debbie; probably I wouldn't be alive, certainly I wouldn't be where I am today, with the hope that I have.

I read somewhere recently – I just remembered it now – that life is like a piano. To hear the music, you have to touch black keys as well as white keys. It is the same as the Russia proverb, 'without salt you won't appreciate sweet.' But I have had too much salt. Until Debbie came, there was only salt in my life, never sweet."

✳

Katya Abramova (25).
Assistant chef and mother to Seryosha, 16 months.

Katya lived in an orphanage about four hours drive from Hortolova, where her brother Max was. These days, Max works in a construction company in Moscow owned by Noel Quinn, an Irishman who has been a huge supporter of To Russia With Love, and who is very fond of Max. Katya had none of the chances Max had, but she had him, and he did everything he could for her. Initially because of him, later because of her own beautiful personality, we did what we could too.

"We grew up like vegetables, with no one caring for us or helping us. Any good way that I have turned out, is thanks to my own efforts, and the efforts of my brother Max. When I feel sad about the way my childhood was, I always think, at least I have something good – I have a wonderful brother who replaced my parents, who cared for me and loved me.

I lived in an orphanage from the age of four, to 18 years old. I don't remember anything about my parents or my life before that. It's like my mind has blocked these things. I suppose they drank, and neglected us, but I don't have any memories of it. I remember being in the car going to the orphanage – I think my mother brought us there herself – but I don't remember anything else about her. It's like an inner shield, a protection. Once in the orphanage, I never saw her again, she never came and visited and we never heard from her.

Sadly, Max was put into in a different orphanage, many hours away. He was in Hortolova, where he made wonderful friends who have become my friends too. At first, he didn't know where to find me. I think it took nearly a year, but he was helped by the Irish who would drive him to different orphanages where he would get out, and walk through huge rooms full of children, searching for me. Eventually, he found me, and from then, he visited when he could. Each time he came, and he would give me his things – good, warm clothes and boots – because what I had was old and worn, and no good for keeping out the cold winters. He knew that when he got back to Hortolova, he would be given more clothes and boots. But he could only come every six months or so.

There were some good things to the orphanage where I lived, but not many. I was taken away on trips when I was very little, by kind families, but mostly we were left very much alone. The hierarchy of the children wasn't good. The older children were mean to the younger ones. They were very tough on us, and the director and staff didn't do much, either to stop them or to help us. And so we grew like vegetables, like a carrot or a cucumber, something left alone, without help.

Everything depended on the child – if you wanted to study, you could do that and they would help you, but if you didn't want to, no one insisted or showed you how to. If you wanted to go and smoke, you could do that and no one stopped you, even when we were very young. So personal motivation is the only thing we had to push us to work and learn, and it's hard to be motivated when you are just seven or eight years old.

There was no one to guide us, no activities, no clubs, no one to say this is good or bad, right or wrong. And so, because I didn't know any better, there was a time when I just went and smoked and didn't study. I didn't try, didn't study, until finally I understood that if I went down that road, I would be entirely lost. So that stimulated me to try hard. Apart from me, no one was going to help me, so I had to do it all myself. I'm an optimist, I want to believe in the best, even when things are so hard. I believe in God, and that any hard things you go through are a test, something you have to go through to come out the other side.

After the orphanage, I wanted to go and study to be a teacher of Russian, but then I discovered that my parents' parental rights had never been formally taken away, so I wasn't technically an orphan, even though I had lived without them, in an orphanage, for 14 years. Because of that, I wasn't eligible for the benefits and assistance that orphans get, so I couldn't study, because I couldn't afford it. Really, I had the worst of both worlds – all the pain and loneliness of having no parents, and none of the benefits I should have had because of that.

Instead of studying, I went to work in the market. I met a boy and he helped me and took me into his house, where his mother cared for me. She worked in the market too, and asked me to go and work with her. So I did, but she had lots of problems with her business. She tried to persuade me to take out loans in my name and get things on credit. I didn't want to do that, and by then the relationship wasn't good either, so I left and went to work in Moscow, where I found work in a mobile phone shop. That's where I met my son's father.

We rented a room and moved in together. His family come from Bryansk, so we visited them, and they were so nice, so kind to me. His mother wanted us to get married and have a baby. It wasn't my idea, but they were so enthusiastic and so welcoming. I thought they could be the family I had never had, and the idea was so beautiful. So he and I went and registered that we wanted to get married, and then I got pregnant.

After that, he changed. He was 26, old enough to be more grown up, but he was unpredictable and moody. In the morning we would wake up and he would be fine, happy, kind to me. By lunchtime, he would be in a terrible temper, saying horrible things to me, saying 'I don't love you any more, I'm getting back with my ex-girlfriend.' He started drinking a lot, and once he came home very drunk and beat me up. I was two months pregnant by then, and because of the beating I got a blood clot in my womb that needed to be operated on. While I was in hospital, this guy stole my passport, in which I was registered to his family's address in Bryansk, because in Russia, everybody needs to be registered to an address, otherwise the State wont do anything for you.

I was discharged from hospital early because I had no insurance for Moscow. In Russia, everything is about insurance! The stitches weren't even taken out yet. So he said, 'go to Bryansk, we will de-register you from my parents' flat, and then I will give you back your passport.' But I didn't have the money to get to Bryansk, so he tore up some of my clothes, threw the rest in the bin, took back all the presents he had given me, and kicked me out of the flat.

There I was, standing by the side of the road in flip-flops, with no food, nowhere to go, I didn't know anybody in Moscow except Max, and I didn't know where he was because the city is too big and I didn't know how to get around it. I didn't even have Max's mobile number. I stood at the side of the road and I closed my eyes and stepped into the traffic, which in Moscow is like walking onto a motorway. But God must have needed me alive, he must have wanted me to have this child, because no car touched me. Drivers were swerving, shouting, swearing, beeping, but they didn't hit me. I kept walking, and at the far side of the road I fell down onto the

Katya Abramova and son Seryosha: "We get up at 5.30am to go to nursery on the bus; he wakes me up and drags me out of bed, because he is so excited to go."

ground. A man came up to me, picked me up, took me to his house and calmed me down, and he helped me to find my brother.

I found Max through Russian Facebook, I hadn't seen him in a few weeks; the last time I saw him I was just newly pregnant and everything was fine, I was so happy with my husband-to-be, and Max was happy for me. Now, everything was different. Max came and got me. He was wonderful, as always. He did everything he could to help me. He brought me to back to Bryansk, to the flat that To Russia With Love keep for their leavers. They call it Peter's Place.

Once back in Bryansk, I met the mother of my ex-boyfriend. She de-registered me from her address, and gave me back my passport. She didn't do a single thing to help me, just said 'don't put him into an orphanage,' about the baby, and that was it.

I still don't understand what happened. They wanted a child so much, my ex, and his mother, and then everything changed, and still I don't know why.

I lived in Peters Place for about a month. Then I moved out, because I couldn't stay there, there were too many people and I was not part of the To Russia With Love leavers programme, so it wasn't right or possible for me to stay. Max's best friend and I rented a studio flat, we had a sofa each, and Max helped me pay for my half. But once I had the baby, I knew I needed to find a place of my own. So I rented a single room in a building, a kind of hostel where there was one toilet for the whole corridor, and one shower for nine floors that was at the bottom of the building and I was at the top. To get to the shower, I had to go down nine flights of stairs, and then back up again.

Seryosha was a big baby, and I couldn't deliver him naturally, so I had a Caesarean section. Because my medical insurance wasn't fully in order, they didn't treat me at the hospital. They just performed the section, and after that they left me on my own. They didn't even disinfect the wound after the first day. The girls who I was in the ward with gave me things – nappies, a shawl, some vests for my baby – and one of the girls, when her husband came to pick her up, came back later and helped me to get out. Her husband carried the baby as if it was his baby, and they drove me to my room. But no official person helped me.

I had nothing at all. No cot, no clothes, not even nappies. I tore up sheets, clothes, anything I could find, to make into nappies. Seryosha was a big baby, and he cried a lot because I wasn't able to feed him enough. He cried and cried, all through the night, and slept very little. I didn't know if I was doing the right things for him, I had no one to ask, no one to show me. I was so worried that I would fail him, and I was tired and in pain and lonely.

I was entirely on my own. Max had to go back to Moscow because of his work, and I had no one to help me. For a month, I lived there without seeing anyone. On one side was an alcoholic woman who ignored me, on the other side was an old lady who wouldn't let me use the sink in the toilet for anything to do with my baby. If I did, she shouted and shouted at me and I couldn't bear it. She watched all the time so it was difficult even to sneak past.

There was no sink in my room, so because of the old woman, to fill a bath for Seryosha, I had wait until he was asleep, then go down all the stairs, fill a bucket, bring it back up again, and boil it, because the water in Bryansk is too harsh and full of chemicals for a baby's skin. Then I would wash myself and our clothes. Because Seryosha was so big, carrying him and picking him up was hard for me. My stitches tore and there was a big hole where they did the section, and it started to become infected and ooze out pus. Every time I knelt down to something with the baby, or if I was walking, or carrying the buggy up the nine floors because it wouldn't fit in the lift, the wound would tear again. It got more and more infected.

The State hospital sent a nurse after a month for an official visit. When she saw the state of my scar, the nurse said 'we have to take you to hospital, this is very serious.' By then, I was close to septicaemia; later I realised I could have died. But at the time, I was in too much of a panic about what would happen to Seryosha if I went into hospital, because they wouldn't let me bring him. I asked, 'what about my baby? There is no one to take him?' They said they would put him in a temporary baby orphanage, but I said no. I was too scared. I didn't know where he would go, how I would find him, if I would get him back. So I said no, I refused to go.

Then I told Max how bad everything was, and he rang Olga who is a director of To Russia With Love in Bryansk, and she came and found me. She brought a massive bag of everything – nappies, clothes, sheets, towels, everything I needed. No one had ever showed me how to care for my son, but now Olga did. She came every day after that. She would bath Seryosha, then clean and disinfect my wound and bandage it until finally it began to heal. She helped and helped. She brought me groceries, bags of things for the baby, and took me to the clinics I needed to go to.

To Russia With Love have a mother and babies programme, to help and support the orphan girls from Hortolova when they have babies, so they do not repeat the mistakes and tragedies of the past. They put me on this programme, even though I was not one of their orphans, because of Max I think, and because they were too kind to turn away.

> "I want to raise my son so that he tells his children 'your grandmother raised me on her own and tried really hard to make a good life for me.' I want to be remembered as someone who, even though I had a hard life and sometimes a bad life, got there in the end and made a success of it."

More than everything, Olga gave me hope. She was my friend, teaching me, showing me, calming me down. She means everything to me. She is like my son's grandmother, and my guardian angel.

If it had not been for Olga and Max, I would have given up, started to drink, given away my baby to be brought up the way I was brought up, in an orphanage. The way things were, I could not have carried on any longer. Now I work, Seryosha is in school, and I have hope. I'm a chef's assistant in the canteen of a business centre. What I really want is to study – sales and management maybe. I want to get my drivers' license, get a better place to live, but at the moment, all the money I earn goes to Seryosha. We get up at 5.30am to go to nursery on the bus; he wakes me up and drags me out of bed, because he is so excited to go.

I want a job I enjoy, where I can wear clothes I like – heels and a skirt, something smart. I want Seryosha to go to school, to bring home good grades, to join clubs like a boxing club; for his day to be busy and full so he has no time to hang around smoking and getting into trouble. I want him to grow up as a strong man who can cope with hardship, who is used to getting up early, working hard and helping women. He is my man, he should help me; I will teach him the right way to be.

I am striving to get to where I want to be in my life, little bit by little bit. Even though things might be really bad now, I know that you have to keep going, that everything will get better. I don't want any more children. This one came with such struggle. I put so much energy and emotion into Seryosha, that I don't want any more. Life is so hard with one child, I don't think I can manage with more. But I want to raise my son so that he tells his children 'your grandmother raised me on her own and tried really hard to make a good life for me.' I want to be remembered as someone who, even though I had a hard life and sometimes a bad life, got there in the end and made a success of it.

There are people who don't have even what I have. My son is healthy and I have a roof over my head. Other people are in the street, begging, with no food. I wake up and I see the sun. I might not have cheese and ham in the fridge, but I have bread.

When I was 17, just before I left the orphanage, I got a letter from my mother. At that time, she was in prison. She wrote that she would like to help us, that she was very proud of us. But she never did anything. Now she is out, she knows she has a grandson but never says that she wants to see him. She just wants somewhere to live, somewhere she can be registered so that she can get some benefit from the State. She doesn't really want to see me, and she's annoyed because I say I won't register her to an address.

But I'm worried that if I do get in contact, my mother will try and come here, she will become dependent on me, and she will be a bad thing in my life and in the life of my son. She won't help us, I know that. I don't want to let love for her into my heart, because I am scared to. I can only just cope – with help – with my son and myself; I don't think I can cope with anything more than that, certainly not with a mother I don't remember and who never cared for me.

I know myself, if I meet her, I will feel sorry for her, and I will let her into my heart, and I think I should not do that. I need to care for my son, and if I let my mother live with us, and she is still drinking and doing the things that got her sent to prison, that is not a good example for him. My mother gave me life, which I am very grateful for, but I can't forgive her for not taking care of us, for giving us up and sending us into this life without protection or help. She might have loved us, as she says, but she didn't show it. She didn't care for us, she didn't help us.

Olga calls me her daughter, and I am happy for that. Recently we were in an office, registering my new address, and a woman said 'oh, look at your beautiful daughter and your wonderful grandson,' and Olga said 'yes!' That made me so, so happy."

✳

Sasha Tzukanov (26).
Sports Coach

Sasha and his two sisters, Vera and Tamara, were sent to Hortolova when Sasha was 10, because his parents were deprived of their parental rights for neglecting and beating the children. From the start, Sasha was an astonishing child, bright, friendly, and wonderfully protective of his sisters. He minded them as if he was their father. These days, he is the sports coach at Hortolova, and we would be lost without him.

"I came to Hortolova in 1997, two days after my tenth birthday. My sisters, Tamara and Vera, were with me. They were younger than me. Before that, we spent about two months in hospital after we were taken away from our parents and the village where we had lived. We weren't sick, but the choice was hospital or the shelter house, and we chose the hospital. There, we just waited, and eventually someone came and brought us to the orphanage.

My parents never came to visit, not the hospital or the orphanage. I have other siblings too, a sister and a brother, older than me. They are the children of my mother, but with a different father, and I never saw them either.

When we lived with our parents, it was in a small village in the woods. At first, those were good times. My parents were working on the farm, we grew vegetables, we had a cow, a horse and chickens. Life was sometimes hard because we didn't have much, but we had enough and we didn't mind working. Even when I was very small, I knew to help with the animals and with growing food. We were a good family, happy together, with the respect of our neighbours and friends. My father was very clever with his hands. All around our village, and villages near by, everyone knew my father because he did things for them. He made and mended doors, windows, sheds, he carved furniture from wood and helped people.

Then the Soviet Union collapsed and everything changed. For my parents, something big changed. I think they gave up. They began to drink all the time, they no longer cooked food or worked on the farm. They let everything go. Those were really hard days for me and my sisters. My parents were drunk every day, it was the purpose of their life, to drink every day, to be drunk, and all they cared about was getting more vodka. My father loved my two sisters, but he never loved me. He would look at me and say, 'I will kill you,' and I think he meant it. He would punch me, slap me, beat me with pieces of wood or anything else that he found. I still have scars all across my head from the beatings he gave me. Sometimes my mother would beat me too. She left her own scars on me.

By the age of seven I could cook, sew and make the fire. Nobody did these things for me, so I did them myself. It was that, or always be without food and warmth. Tamara helped me and together we took care of Vera who was the youngest.

We had no gas or electricity so Tamara and I would go to the woods to gather wood for the fire. I was working as well, from the age of six or maybe seven, with my father, herding cows every day. Usually my father would take a bottle of vodka, he would drink it and fall asleep, so I took care of the cows instead of him. It was better for me that he was asleep rather than awake. I didn't mind work, I did mind being beaten. Nobody paid me, but the owners would give me some milk, maybe a piece of bread. If I had bread, I was happy. Mostly I ate sunflower seeds, wild strawberries, anything I could find in the fields and woods.

Sometimes I forgot to take water with me when I was minding the cows, so I would drink river water.

All my father ever told me was that he hated me and wanted to kill me. When he was drunk, I would run away, because I was so scared of what he could do. And if I didn't, he was likely to shout 'get out of here!' and then I would have to go anyway, even in wintertime, usually without shoes because we had no money for shoes. In my bare feet, I would stay outside in temperatures of –20 because I was too scared of what he would do to me if I went home.

Other times he would order me, 'go and get me cigarettes.' I had no money, but I would go around the whole village asking, 'can you give me a cigarette please?' The first few times, people did, but after a while, they stopped. They had their own problems, their own families, their own difficulties, they couldn't look out for us as well. We weren't the only children in that village who were beaten and neglected. If I went home without cigarettes, my father would punch and punch me. Even if she wanted to, my mother couldn't protect me. He would punch and punch her too. Many times I remember seeing her with her head cut and bleeding, falling to the ground or staggering around because he hit her so hard.

School was the best place for me to be in those days, and I loved it. I was good at my lessons and worked hard, and my teacher was so kind to me. By the time I was seven or eight years old, that was the only kindness I had in my life apart from my sisters. Every day I walked 5km each way to get to this school, which was in a different village. My teacher knew about the kind of life I had at home, everybody knew about everyone in those villages, there were no secrets. And my parents didn't try to hide what they were doing. Everyone knew that they were drunk and we were hungry and neglected. I always came to school dirty, without shoes or coat, with no food. Often my mind would not be working because I was so hungry, or tired. Eventually, my teacher wrote to the local district administration and the social workers decided to take us away.

And so, in 1997, the three of us came to Hortolova. We were lucky that we were put in the same orphanage, but in those days, before the Irish, Hortolova was very different. It was a place where only the strong survived, the weak were broken and lost. There were 170 children in those days, mostly running wild. We robbed any dachas we could find, we broke in and stole food, because we were starving, so the local people who lived around the orphanage hated us.

To eat, all we ever had was beetroot, and a really cheap kind of soup, basically water with a few pieces of potato in it. The windows of the orphanage were broken and the wind and cold came in. The radiators didn't work, neither did the toilets, which were really disgusting. There was no soap, no towels, no toothbrushes, but I didn't know anything about such things in those days. I was just trying to work out what was this place we were sent to, and how to survive there.

At first I really missed my father and mother. Every night going to sleep, I would think about my mother and wonder when she would come for us. My parents were not good for us, I know that now, but when I was small I didn't really understand. After all, even though they hit me and shouted, they did give me some food and, sometimes, some care. I suppose they gave what they could give.

Mainly though, we didn't know anything else. We didn't know how other children lived – I could see that other children were different to us, that they had better food, better clothes, a better

"I still have scars all across my head from the beatings he gave me. Sometimes my mother would beat me too. She left her own scars on me."

house, nobody beating them – but in my heart and my soul, I didn't feel it. The way we lived seemed normal to me, and to my sisters.

Gradually I realised that even though Hortolova was not a good place, it was actually a better place than being with my parents. At least I had some food and shoes, even if they were old, cheap shoes. I could go to school without walking for 10km. My sisters were with me, and because I was strong for my age, I didn't get bullied by the older boys.

It was hard to be the littlest in Hortolova in those days. Luckily, I was in the middle group for size, but the older boys would still demand that we gave them our bread. If we didn't, they beat us up. That happened to me a few times, so then I decided to try to make friends with the older boys. I was good at sport, and that helped, I got friendly with some of them, and after that nobody touched me. Once that happened, it meant I was able to protect my sisters too so nobody touched them either. Every day, I was running around finding Tamara and Vera, making sure they were ok, that everybody minded them and looked after them and didn't bully them. The other kids in the orphanage couldn't understand how we three were so close. Other brothers and sisters would come to the orphanage and never speak to each other again. I think that is one of the tragedies, but for us, we were used to caring for each other, minding each other, and we continued to do it in the orphanage, same as at home.

I don't really remember when Debbie, Trish and the Irish came for the first time, but I remember the small changes that started to happen immediately, even before all the big rebuilding work. I remember that the Irish bought me the first ice cream I ever had in my life. I will never forget that! They gave us toothpaste – Colgate – and soap, I think those were the first things. Good towels because all we had were worn old rags. It didn't happen overnight, but bit by bit I could see more and more changes. They gave us good shoes, not the broken cheap ones we had before.

We all tried to be with the volunteers all the time. The Russian carers were very stressed, and underpaid, they had other problems in their lives besides us but we felt the Irish cared about us and loved us, they had time to care, they were there because they wanted to be. They were like mothers. At night, these volunteers would come and kiss us before we went to sleep. No one had ever done that to me before; it was the first time such a nice thing ever happened. At first, I ran away, I didn't know what hugs or kisses were, and I was scared. But when I understood and got used to it, it was lovely.

I was so interested to be with these Irish volunteers, because before them, I never heard anyone speak anything except Russian. I didn't know that English existed. In my small village, I never learned anything about the outside world. Not at the orphanage either. In fact, when I first went there, I was so much better at school than my classmates that I was shocked by how bad the level of education was. And I was shocked at the way the children would talk to their teachers. I was the best in the class, and I was chosen as class leader from the first year I arrived, in fifth class, through to the end. Every year the pupils had the chance to choose someone else, but they never did.

Those years after the Irish came were the best of my life. Once they arrived, everything was better. We had more help, more love. We knew they cared about us, crazy as it seemed at first that anyone would care, we saw that they did. We watched everything as it happened. When Debbie came on her first 10 or even 20 visits, she would sit with us quietly, and often she cried. We knew that she cared so much for us. During every visit, all us children would be running around madly, calling "Debbie, Debbie, Debbie," looking in every room, trying to find her. When we knew she was due a visit, we would all clean our rooms, clean our clothes, make Hortolova look as nice as possible. She changed everything for us children.

At first in Hortolova, we had no balls, no sports equipment, no TV, no computers. Once things began to change, we had everything we needed, and then we began to show what we were capable of. Every year there was competition between all the orphanages in various sports – football, volleyball, basketball, running, skiing. Every year, Tamara and I entered the competitions, and every year we won. No matter what the sport, we were always the best. Even when we entered competitions with non-orphanage schools, for family children, we still won, even though they had much better equipment. We won cups, medals, trophies; enough to fill the cabinets and make all of Hortolova proud.

After leaving, I went to university in Bryansk, where I studied English and law, but it was too hard, just too much work. So I left for technical college, to study to be a driving instructor. I was there for four years, and made really good friends, one of them took me in and fed me when I didn't have enough money in college, and is now married to my sister Tamara. Vera is at university, studying PE, and works part time in a shopping centre, selling dresses. My sisters and I are still very close.

These days I am back at university, doing a distance-learning course, and I work for To Russia With Love, fulltime. I'm the sports coach at Hortolova, and I'm trying to develop the teams, bring them back to the glory days when I was there. These days, I think the kids have too many toys, too many computers. They don't practise as hard as we did – we got up at 6am and trained before school, then more after school and in the evenings. But recently the football team took third place in a tournament, which is not bad. To Russia With Love paid for the bus to take us there; first we asked the orphanage director for money for the bus, but she said no, it wasn't in the budget. The Irish bailed us out again. They still buy all the footballs; I'd say we go through one every few weeks.

My father died in 2000, when I was still in Hortolova. He died from too much vodka, he drank so much that his liver finally gave up. Nobody told me when he died, but when Debbie came and heard that, she decided that I needed to know, and so, a year after his death, she helped me, Tamara and Vera to go back to the village where we spent our childhood. So we went home, for the first time in years, for one night, and we saw his grave. Standing there, I felt sad, trying to understand what had happened to all of us. We didn't see my mother on that trip because by then she had moved to Bryansk. In fact, we never saw her again; in 2008, she died also from vodka. Once my father died, she started drinking even more, all day, all night, until finally it killed her.

We didn't have a good early life, my sisters and I, and if we had not been lucky to be in the right orphanage – the one Debbie and the Irish stepped into – I wonder what would have happened to us? Certainly nothing as good as this."

Pasha Potemkin (26).
Construction worker

Pasha spent his earliest years at the same baby orphanage as Zina. When he was seven, he was fostered by a Russian man who mistreated him terribly until eventually Pasha ran away. He never stopped looking for Zina and eventually, through pure chance, he met someone from the To Russia With Love team, and we were able to help him.

"My mum was in prison when I was born. I don't know why she was sent there. She delivered me in the prison and was allowed to keep me with her for a year. Then I was transferred to a baby orphanage, and I never saw my mum again, I don't know what happened to her.

The baby orphanage was the same one where Zina was, a place called Klintsy. I liked it, it was a very good place. I had my friends there, I was well cared for and happy. Zina was my best friend, we were inseparable, always did everything together. We played together, sat together, when we got in trouble, we even got in trouble together. We protected each other and showed each other the kindness and gentleness that children need.

Zina and I went to Ireland on the same trip, all those years ago. Just like her, I met an Irish family who loved me dearly. I stayed with them for a month and we got very close, so it was very painful to leave them come back. I know they loved me, but they were not as decisive as Debbie, who moved so quickly to keep Zina. My family let me go back, even though I know they wanted to keep me.

Back in the orphanage, without Zina I was very lonely. Then, when I was seven, some Russian people came and visited me. I didn't understand much or pay attention to them, although I know they told me something about living in a village. In fact, I was fostered by this Russian family, and stayed with them for 10 years. From the moment they took me away from the orphanage, my life was terrible, and horrible. Getting used to any new people would have been difficult, but in this case, because of who they were, it was catastrophic.

They took me although they had no experience with children, and no foster training. The man had a history of violence and had spent time in prison; even so, they let him foster a seven-year-old boy. He had no idea, and couldn't have cared less, about how to raise a child. For him, this was a business decision – take a child who was old enough to work, be paid extra money from the State for taking this child, and then ignore every bit of the caring process that should go into raising a child.

For him, I was free labour. Better, the State actually paid him for this extra labour. I grew vegetables, kept the house and sheds clean, tended the garden, minded the chickens and pigs. I helped to build garages, sheds, storage houses and a sauna. If it had just been a question of hard work, I wouldn't have minded so much, because I learned many skills, and because I was working hard, I was distracted from sad moments and thoughts because there was always so much to do. In fact, I can thank that man for forcing me to learn so many new skills, because now I use them to earn my living. He taught me well.

But that man was cruel to me. From the moment he fostered me, my perception of childhood was just punches, kicks and insults. He beat me, mocked me and sometimes starved me, and

Pasha Potemkim: "Today I am very happy. I have a good life. I'm married to a beautiful girl, I have a daughter who is nearly one."

the women around him were usually no better. During the ten years I was in that terrible house, there were at least four different women. For a child, that meant four different people to try to get used to, sometimes to bond with, only for them to go away and never see them again. I was so lonely and there was no affection in my life, so if any of them showed me even a tiny bit of kindness, I would feel warm towards her. Then they would fight, and she would go away, and that bit of warmth would go with her.

The last woman who lived with him during my years there was the worst. She was there the longest time, and she was very cruel. I was about 10 when she came first. To me, she seemed like a wild person from a

> "My life was terrible. Even now, I cannot talk about the things that happened to me in that house. I was even jealous of children living in orphanages. To me, that was the best life I had known."

forest – untidy, dirty, smelly, she couldn't speak properly, and she had headlice, that I then got as well. She had three children by different men, and one of the children, her youngest son, came with her to live with us.

It was so hard to see this smelly stranger come and ruin the house where I had worked so hard, and everyone praised her and ignored me.

Even before she came, I was like a second-hand child who no one paid any attention to, but after she and her son arrived, I was pushed even further out. She wanted her son to be loved, protected and cared for, to be first in all things. There was nothing left for me at all.

School was my only escape and refuge from the terrible things that happened at home. Being there, safe, were my most precious moments – nobody cursed me, hit me or insulted me when I was at school. I wasn't very successful at my studies, but that was the happiest place for me. In fact it was the only happy place; for half of each day I could be left alone there. But then I would have to go back to them again, and all the trouble would start the second I walked in the door.

That woman was so determined to be cruel to me. She made it her business to know all my weak points – for example, I hate barley, so barley was the only thing she gave me to eat. If she knew I hated a particular insult more than others, that was the one she would choose to use. In everything she did, her goal was to humiliate me and drive me away.

As time passed and I grew bigger and stronger, more able to stand up for myself, I wasn't a kind child. I suppose no one could have expected it of me, and I wasn't. I spent all my time thinking about killing – killing her, killing myself, killing her son, killing my foster father.

As far as I remember, I was a kind and affectionate boy when I was very young and in the orphanage. I think I was gentle and cared for other people. But that changed when I was surrounded by

"Our plan was to try and renovate the orphanage, make it into a safe, warm, homely place, with smaller, brighter rooms and better facilities."

"Our plan – and we are very good at it – is to break that cycle, to give them the self-esteem, the support, the belief they need to make a success of their lives."

"We never turn our backs on the children. For as long as they need us, we're there. Even if they end up in prison. And yes, it has happened. But only once. Generally, we are unbelievably successful at keeping them out – when you consider that the national average for orphan boys who go on to prison is 30-odd percent – our record is remarkable."

"Our orphans are in no-mans' land, and no man wants to know them. Locals don't give to orphanages, they don't walk in on a Sunday with a bag of sweets for the kids or even a few pairs of socks.

"I think our children, in Hortolova, feel safe and are safe, because we are there all the time, minding them, listening to them, watching over them. There is a spotlight on them and I think we've made them safe because of that."

"If you look at the UN Declaration of the Rights of the Child, it's such a beautiful thing – "The child ... needs love and understanding. He shall, wherever possible, grow up in the care and under the responsibility of his parents ... a child of tender years shall not, save in exceptional circumstances, be separated from his mother."

"Our children grow up in a world where they are absolutely alone. I still wonder, looking at our children, how you get through life without love? Without comfort? Without kindness? Without somebody to rub your back when your feeling low?"

Top: Anna and Maria from the English Nursery School, who bring so much love, vital supplies and gorgeous gifts to the children.

Right: Russian TV star Andrei Malakhov who has been a fantastic supporter of To Russia With Love.

Above: The wonderful author Marian Keyes is a long time supporter of ours , she shops in "With Love" regularly and recently donated a wardrobe of beautiful clothes, shoes and bags.

Far right: Debbie in Hortolova with a happy child.

"Even among Russia companies, it is becoming a bit trendy, now, to help orphanages. Sixteen years ago when I started, it wasn't trendy at all. Frankly, it was like working with rats. All I heard was honest bafflement – 'why do you want to help these children?' But the psyche is gradually, grindingly, changing. The current political situation is, sadly, another huge challenge for us to cope with, as Corporate Social Responsibility is not high on people's agendas right now."

so much brutality, ignorance and cruelty. I became more like them than I ever wanted to be. One day I realised that I had become a monster, with terrible thoughts running constantly through my head; thoughts of murder, suicide, violence. I wanted to make those people suffer as much as they had made me suffer for so many years.

I was so jealous of children living in orphanages. To me, that was the best life I had known. Orphanage children had shelter every day and night, they were never sent out barefoot into the snow, they were not insulted in the way that I was insulted, mistreated in the way that I was mistreated. Even now, I cannot repeat all the horrible things that happened to me in that family, because they were so bad. If you are sober, you can't even think about them. No body knows all the details of it, because I have never been able to tell. I cannot say the words to describe those things, but I know what they did to me.

Her son was younger than me and not as strong. I bullied him every day, as much as I was able to without being caught. When I could get away with it, I would hit him with my full strength. I wanted to kill him, but he had the protection of his mother, and my stepfather never protected me from her.

One day, there was a final incident that brought everything to a head. I was about 15 at that time. I pushed the son by accident when we were working on something. Now, I had pushed and punched him many times before, but this time I didn't do it on purpose. But she saw me and she rushed at me and pushed me onto some rocks. I got so angry that I lost control, and I beat the shit out of her. In those moments, I was ready to kill her. My stepfather was right there, he stood watching and laughing, enjoying the show, this savage spectacle in front of him.

Even though I beat her she kept insulting me, so I picked up a sack full of rocks that lay beside me, and I was ready to hit her with it, to finally kill her. Something stopped me, thank God. Instead I ran away, I had a friend living nearby, who was a wood-cutter in the forest, and together we decided to leave that place. I went back home, took all my paper work – my passport, my school certificate, everything I needed, and he and I left together. We went to Bryansk, rented an apartment and I started to work, trying to earn money, to earn a living. I entered a vocational school, which was easy to do because I was an orphan, so I was given accommodation in the hostel. I studied to be a welder, and I tried to leave those horrible things behind me.

But it was hard. If the only thing you have ever seen is hatred and insults, it is very hard to be any other way, to find anything better inside yourself. I was not a nice person I think in those days. I had so much anger and hatred in me, they were part of me for a very long time, I only managed to begin to get rid of them about three years ago.

Strangely, what began to change me was committing a crime. I was nearly convicted of fighting, because in those days, I would go out and look for fights, to get rid of my aggression which was too much for me to cope with. My solicitor was free, from State aid, and he didn't care about me because I was an orphan and wasn't bothering to do his best for me. When I realised that everything was going to end very badly for me, I decided to say something for myself. I stood up in the court and started to speak. I told the judge the story of my life, and that I understood now that I had to try harder, make an effort to have a different life. This saved me.

Telling the story out loud made me look at it again, and I decided then, I have to forgive those people, forgive everything that they did to me, and everything that they didn't do for me, because otherwise it will destroy me. So I let it go. After that, it became easier for me to keep going. There are still days when the past comes back, when it seems as if I will never ever be able to get rid of it, that it will be part of me for the rest of my life, but there are more days when I know that I am going to be ok.

Around that same time, fate brought something so good into my life. It was 2007, September, and I was in the hostel of my college. There were a couple of school leavers from Hortolova starting in that college, and Ina, a staff member from To Russia With Love, was with them, helping to settle them in.

The guy I shared my room with was like me – a bit older than the other students, stronger, more developed. We were the leaders on the floor. So this girl, Ina came and talked to us. She asked us if we would look after the child from Hortolova, make sure he was ok and that no one bullied him. She was a really stunning girl. Frankly, I didn't really listen to what she was saying, I just stared at her. It's funny; if she hadn't been so pretty, this next bit of my story would never have happened!

Anyway, I asked her to come for a tea in my room the next time she was at the college. She said, 'I wont have tea, but I will come and see the room.' I think she was just being polite. Anyway, I didn't care, I was glad she was coming. I cleaned the room and everything, made it look nice. On the wall was a picture of Zina and Debbie, one of the very few photos I had. I had carried it every-where with me, ever since I left the baby orphanage. Zina had brought it back with her after her trip to Ireland, and when she left to live with Debbie permanently, she gave the photo to me. I had kept it with me always.

Ina was shocked when she saw the picture of Debbie. She said 'this is my boss!' How do you know her? Tell me your story?' So I told her a little bit, and she was interested. I told her that I had been searching for Zina for years and years, in vain. We had no friends in common, no one I could go to and ask. I didn't know where any of my classmates from that orphanage were because I had been fostered and they had all gone in different directions. Some had been adopted to America, the rest were split up and sent to different institutions, I didn't know where to start looking to find them. Ina knew that Debbie had an adopted daughter called Zina, although she had never met her, and she said 'Ok, I know a Zina, let me check it out and I will let you know.' So I waited and waited for a text message from her, every day. I was so anxious, I was shaking, praying that the text would come and that it would be the right answer.

I suppose that seems strange, about a person who I hadn't seen since I was seven? But my favourite moments of my childhood happened in that baby orphanage. I loved it there. Everything in my life had been bad and ugly from the moment I left, and so I looked back all the time to these sweet, lovely flashbacks from the happiest part of my past. It was the one place I felt I was loved, and Zina was the person who I identified most of that with.

I was in class when a text message finally arrived from Ina. In it she said 'yes, I can confirm that it is the same girl, and she has been searching for you for years also.' Right there, I went to pieces. The strong, grown-up young man I had become went instantly back to a child. I was all over the place crying. I couldn't stop.

Ina arranged a meeting with Debbie, and from the beginning there was a strong connection between us, something between me and her from the first moment. I have to say, Debbie and To Russia With Love turned me around completely. It is not an exaggeration to say they changed my life. Before them, I was driven into a corner with my life. I didn't know what to do, how to make anything good happen for myself. I wasn't proactive, just passively taking all the bad things that came to me.

Until Debbie and To Russia With Love, the only friends I had were criminals and bullies. These were the people who were willing to be my friends, other Russians didn't want to know me, and I didn't feel anything in common with normal people. Through Debbie, I began to make new friends. I liked the people she brought over from Ireland, and the Russian people she found to work with her. For me, they were a completely new type of people, interesting. Meeting them was like an eye-opener to a new kind of life, a new way to live, with love, warmth, good friendships, the kind of comfortable and trustful relations that I had never had before. I learned that people could care for me, something I never knew. I cherish these friendships and relationships. These people support me all the time, through everything that happens, I know I can trust them and rely on them.

Debbie offered to put me on the TRWL Leaver programme, but I wasn't comfortable saying yes to that. I rejected the offer, but they helped me anyway, unofficially. She helped me financially a lot, she helped with my accommodation, she put me on the Peter's Place programme so I could live there when I didn't have anywhere else to go. When I had no job, no money, no hope, she gave me belief that I could do something with my life. What changed was friendship. More than the money, the programmes, even the trips to Ireland, it was the attitude – knowing that someone had started to care for me. I don't know how to describe how much Debbie has influenced my life, but she has, in so many ways.

She brought me to Ireland at the end of 2007, and at last I met

Zina again. I had waited so long for this to happen, but now we were adults. It was different, so awkward, not what I expected. I had expected hugs, tears, the same instant bond that we used to have, but she was so grown up, so Westernised. We had grown up in completely different worlds. It was very sad to accept that, but I realised quickly enough. I was shy, very closed, because I was thinking about everything that had happened since we last met. We didn't even talk that much, because we didn't speak the same language anymore. It was hard to accept that.

I went back to Russia and we continued writing to each other. I didn't have relatives or family or many friends, so I kept writing to her. I didn't have anyone else. I don't know what I wanted from the relationship, except that I wanted it to be the same between Zina and me, for us to be together the way we were when we were children.

Two years passed, and we met again on Malokov's show, the biggest chat show in Russia, watched by 50 million people. Malokov was doing a story on Zina and Debbie and To Russia With Love, and they asked me to go on and talk about my time in the baby orphanage. I prepared a speech, about childhood, about friendship, but when I came out and saw Zina, I decided, 'I'll say what I feel – it's now or never!' So I gave a speech that was completely different to the one I prepared, I proposed to her.

She didn't say yes. I suppose she couldn't. She said she was settled in Ireland, she had her life, her friends, she didn't want to leave. It wasn't what I hoped to hear, and so we stopped talking. Then I found out she had met somebody, she had a boyfriend. I didn't have anybody to wait for anymore, so I found a girlfriend as well. I got married, she got engaged. And from then, we were just good friends. I just hope, whoever she is with, that it is a good love.

That he will care for her with real love not just words. I wish the best things for her.

Today I am very happy. I have a good life. I'm married to a beautiful girl, I have a daughter who is nearly one. I recently bought an apartment, I have a job I love and good friends.

When I was on that trip to Ireland to see Zina, Debbie found the family I had stayed with when I was a child, and arranged a meeting. It was wonderful to see them again. They were the same as ever – kind and loving. I discovered then that they had really wanted to adopt me after that visit. They went to Klintsy orphanage three years in a row trying to trace me and find news of me, but they couldn't find anything. The information was not kept well – I think because the man I was fostered to had been in prison, and so the staff didn't want a record of it. When the Irish family realised they couldn't find me, they were very upset. But when I heard they had wanted me, I was heartbroken.

All I could think was, 'why did so many bad things happen to me? Why did Zina get so lucky and I didn't?' I just went down, into the mud. If I had been luckier, I would have had real parents, people I could call mum and dad, and I would have been so happy. It didn't work out like that for me.

I know there are worse stories than mine, but I still think about the reasons why the good things didn't happen for me as a child. That Irish family wanted to adopt me so badly, and it is only by evil chance that they didn't. There is no answer to why this happened, and why my life was so terrible for so long.

Except that I have some kind of answer, because now is good, and I believe the future will be good."

✳

Misha Serdyukov (26).
Interpreter

Misha is one of our greatest success stories. A smart boy, he drove himself very hard to succeed at the Lycium, an academically distinguished school where he went to study. He finished university and now has a job as translator for a private business client. He was always one of our loveliest, most motivated boys and it is a joy to see how well he is doing in life.

"I lived in an orphanage from the time I was very small. I don't really remember anything before it, or how I came to be there, although when I was older I found out some things about my background that I will tell later.

The first orphanage I was in was Klintsy, where I stayed until I was eight years old. I liked it there, I was happy and it was a good time. I was interested in everything, and the carers soon discovered that I was clever at doing things. I could fix the TV when it stopped working, and I was good at making the traditional Russia dolls and painting them in black, gold and red. I enjoyed doing those things, learning and making things.

Once I got too old for Klintsy orphanage, I was moved, with my class, to Hortolova. We were all so scared when we were being moved, because we

Misha Serdyukov: "For all the kids like me who never met their families, it was so good to know there was somebody, somewhere who thought about us".

didn't know where we would go. We were happy where we were and didn't want to leave and didn't know what was waiting for us at the other end of the journey.

In fact, what was waiting, at first anyway, was a horrible place to live. Everything in Hortolova was old, broken, rusty and smelly. There were ten of us kids to a room, with just one small wardrobe for all our clothes so that the clothes lay in heaps on the ground and were never clean. It was not a good orphanage, the atmosphere was not good. The carers didn't care for us, they let us run wild. I don't remember that I learned anything when I was there first, because no one took the trouble to teach us, and there were not any board games or paints or crafts to do.

I remember so well the day Debbie first arrived. She came to visit Zina's classmates – I was one of them – and we were excited to see this strange person. Her arrival made that an unusual day, it became colourful, because usually we didn't get visits. Also, she brought sweets! I remember, we were all collected in a special area to meet her, and every one of us went up to her again and again, from all sides, to try and take more sweets. At that time there was no good food given to us in Hortolova, We were always hungry, and had never seen so many sweets in our lives. We crowded and pressed around her, trying to grab what we could.

But I wanted to say thank you as well. I must have been ten years old. I drew a picture, a dragon I think, and gave it to Debbie as a present, to remember about me. I didn't think she would come back, but I was grateful for what she had done that day.

This was our first real meeting. I understand now more about what she saw there on that day – the way we looked, the way we were, what she thought when she saw us and the way we lived – and I can understand the way she reacted. She knew it needed to be changed, and from that moment on, she began to do everything she could. Every time she came back, it was a celebration day. Other days were grey days.

The orphanage became so that you would never recognise it. To Russia with Love started to rebuild. First the canteen, which was a small terrible place, where we ate from metal plates with spoons, never knives and forks. It looked and felt like a prison. You ate your food and you were always hungry, but you could never ask for any more. There wasn't more, and there would be trouble if you asked. Anyway the food was so disgusting that even though we were hungry, we didn't really want to eat more of it. When the work was completed, the canteen became bigger, more colourful, more interesting to be in; there was even a special room at the side where we could celebrate our birthdays with the group, and be popular once a year. Before Debbie, we never had birthdays.

During that first year, I remember a big truck came to the orphanage, and out of it appeared so many different things for us – clothes, food, toys, books, games. All of this helped us a lot; Hortolova became a place where we could try new things, find out interesting information. We tried different dishes; after eating the same thing every day for years, it was so exciting to have something new that we didn't know.

Debbie found us sponsor families in Ireland who would send us letters, cards, photos. Every year the families would send us a Christmas gift. We used to wait so eagerly, to see what was inside the present. For all the kids like me who never met their families, it was so good to know there was somebody, somewhere who thought about us. The idea that somebody wants to make you a little bit happier, to let you have something that normal children living with a family have, but you don't, that is a wonderful feeling.

It does make you happier. Even if you never see them, and some of us never met our sponsor families, we knew they were there and they cared. I used to write back, to thank them. I wanted to meet them so badly, to see what they were like and say thank you for the difference they made. All of us children would wait for their letters and talk to each other about our sponsor families; what they were doing, if they had a new cat or a car, had been on holiday or if someone had a birthday in their family. It was so interesting and unusual for us to have something like this to talk about, a connection with the big world that wasn't Russia.

From childhood, I was always alone. I never had any family that I remember, so I could not compare anything with the experience of having a sponsor family. From the beginning, I had nobody to visit or take me out, no sisters or brothers, not even a grandmother. That was a constant source of upset for me. Nearly all the other children in the orphanage had someone. Maybe not a mother or a father, but perhaps an aunt, a grandmother, a sister; somebody to care, to come and visit them, to take them out sometimes. It made me so sad to see the luckier children being visited or collected by their family. I would try and get away, go where I didn't have to see them.

In my life, it was always just me, from the start. So I never understood how upset some children would be when they first came to the orphanage. They would wait and wait for someone to come, they would cry for the family they had left, who they missed. Often no one came. I suppose for me in some ways it was easier because I didn't expect anything. But it was sad too. I always wanted somebody to come for me and see where I was, what I was doing. To ask for me and wait to know the answer. But there was no one.

Because of that, I cared so much about my sponsor family, and I made very good friends with the volunteers Debbie brought from Ireland. All day every day I knocked at the door of the flat where they stayed, asking for paper, scissors, glue, something to eat; anything at all, just to be with them. From that interest came the first motivation for me to start learning English. I was so interested in the way these volunteers were, the way they looked, they way they smelled, the way they spoke to each other.

When I was in the 9th form, Debbie organised a trip to Ireland with a group of us, she called it Operation Vacation. We were meant to stay for two weeks, but Jean McCarthy who I stayed with and who I got on great with, asked me to stay longer - a whole month in Ireland. I had such a great time. I was serious about learning English by then, so it was real practise for me. By the time I left, I spoke half-English, half-Russian, but the English half was getting stronger.

In all, I went to Ireland seven times. Debbie invited me to stay with her, to meet her family, and on one trip she asked me to be the guest speaker at a dinner for 300 people in the Four Seasons hotel. This was scary, but I wanted to do it. I wanted to tell those people everything Debbie had done for me and the other children, and I was proud that she asked me.

By then I was in Lycium, studying very hard.

Once everything was rebuilt in the orphanage and we lived in better conditions, Debbie began to turn her attention to our education and what we might do with our lives. The school programme in Hortolova was too easy for me, and the people in TRWL recognised this. Debbie asked me, 'would you like to go to a really good school to study? It will be hard, but I want you to try it because it will be good for you.' I was surprised because I didn't know there was any possibility to go to a better school, and I was scared. I had never been anywhere except Klintsy orphanage and Hortolova orphanage in my life, except for a few trips to Ireland where I was taken great care of. But I said 'yes, I would like to.' I was 12 years old and I understood this was a chance for me, and that I needed to take it.

From the start, it was very difficult. To be in that school you had to know a lot about every subject, and the other children knew so much more than me. They had a much better education, they were family children and their parents supported them and helped them. Even for family children it was a hard school to get into, and only the very cleverest succeeded in getting in and staying there. Half the children were from really rich families, the other half weren't, but they were at least from families, and that was already more than I had. As well as getting used to the school and the work, I had to get used to a new place to live, new people. It was definitely scary. But I said yes, and I meant yes.

TRWL bought a suit, because in that school they have a uniform, and even that was strange for me. I had never worn anything like that before.

The first year was so difficult. The levels of knowledge were so different between me and the rest of the students. At the start, I thought, 'I won't be here for long,' but I also told myself not to give up. The pressure was huge – lessons started at 8am, finished at 4pm, and, because I was behind in some subjects, I asked those teachers to give me extra lessons. They knew where I came from, and they wanted me to succeed, so they were prepared to help. With their help, I studied further every day from 4pm-6pm, and then again from 6pm-8pm. And after that, it was time for homework, usually about two more hours. It was very intense, but that was what I needed to do, otherwise I would not have been able to continue there.

Those first six months were the hardest. After that, it started to become a little easier. The teachers began to believe that I could do it, and slowly, I did too. I stayed in the hostel at the Lycium where I was looked after and fed, so all I had to do was study, study, study.

Some of the other kids helped me as well. I suppose I was interesting for them – someone new, from a different kind of background. Also, I played a lot of sport. Football, volleyball, basketball, everything, and I was good, so they wanted to be on my team. In fact, sport is what helped me to communicate with them. This was the point where we came together. They had everything and I had nothing, but in sport we connected and became friends.

It was so hard, but I understood that if I wanted this to work out, I had to work hard. I tried to find ways to make things easier, but no matter what I did, it was still difficult to reach the level I needed to be at.

At one stage, Debbie actually wanted to take me away from that school, because she decided it was too much for me. She thought I was killing myself to succeed there, and that the difference between my situation and that of the other kids was just too much, too unfair, and that I shouldn't be expected to compete with them.

They were all highly academic, rich, they had everything, and people to help them constantly. She was right that I was highly stressed and exhausted, but I was determined not to give up. I learned there that if you want something, you really have to go for it.

And Debbie helped me a lot, with copybooks, clothes, sports gear, but also with my confidence. There was always someone from TRWL to check on me, available for me to talk to, ready to help in any way they could.

The second year was much easier. All the teachers were proud of me, of the way I was studying, and I knew then that I could do it, that the worst was behind me. I learned so much there, about school, but also about what is possible in life if you make yourself work and try hard.

I finished the Lycium with very good marks. In this country, if you are an orphan, once you get decent marks, you can get into university, but I got the highest possible score, and could go anywhere.

At first I thought of Moscow University, because it is the best, but in the end the idea was too daunting. Moscow is such a massive city, especially for an orphan. So instead I went to Bryansk State Technical University, where I studied maths and computer programming. This is the flagship course of the university and very hard to get into. I was intensely proud of myself – that I did it, I got it. After everything, I had something to show for all my hard work. I felt that I wanted to keep moving, keep achieving, and I knew that I could.

And I was proud too that the people who cared about me were pleased. Debbie was so proud of me, and that made me very happy. I know that if I had stayed in the orphanage school, I couldn't have done this. The good things that have happened for me, they are not just because of me – it was support from Debbie and the good Irish carers who came and gave us hope.

However, now I also had to deal with real life. No more canteen to feed me or people to look after me. I needed somewhere to live, I needed to work out how to find time to shop and cook for myself, as well as time to study for the course. I know that sounds easy, but after a life of being told exactly when and where to do everything, it is very hard for orphan children to manage these things.

Debbie helped me to find a place to live, an apartment in a lady's house who would also cook me one meal a day. That was practise for living on my own, a gradual transition. After that, I moved into Peter's Place, where I lived with some of the other leavers from Hortolova who were going to the university and technical college. That was great. We were all back together again, helping each other, working out how to do things, how to get used to our new world.

Once a week, someone from TRWL would come to the flat to see how we were getting along, what we needed. They helped us constantly, with extra money, with advice, recommendations. We knew there were people to give us support and help us, and that was a very good feeling. So many orphans, after they leave the institutions where they have been brought up, live in a very bad way.

They have never experienced freedom before, always routine and timetables, and having it makes them go crazy. They think they can do anything they want, so they steal, they drink, they don't go to lessons, they fall into bad company, and often as a result, they get kicked out of college, which is often the beginning of a long slide into misery for them.

In Peter's Place, we had very strict rules, of what to do and what not to do, but they were rules that we agreed with and that we wanted. I believe that if you are shown the right direction, you will follow it. So we did. No parties, keep the flat clean, no inviting other friends to stay there, regular study hours, being quiet and considerate of each other, that kind of thing.

Each year we were expected to find a job for the summer so that we could gradually get used to making our own way, and not rely always on others. Working and earning our own money, even if it wasn't very much, taught us that we were finally adults, not children to be looked after all the time. We began to learn to think for ourselves; with support initially, but gradually with more and more independence.

After five years I finished university. Most of the time I worked as well as studying, because I needed the money, and at one job waiting tables, I met a girl who I am now married to. Last June I finished my thesis. I wrote it at night, and worked as a personal trainer during the day. While there, I met an English guy who I trained, who works for a company based here. We got on very well, and he asked if I wanted to work for him, as a translator, so that is

"I was intensely proud of myself. After everything, I had something to show for all my hard work. I felt that I wanted to keep moving, keep achieving, and I knew that I could. And I was proud too that the people who cared about me were pleased."

what I am doing now.

In Russia, there is a rule that once you finish university as an orphan, the government will give you an apartment, somewhere permanent to live, where you don't pay rent, only the bills. In theory, it is a good idea, but in practise, it doesn't work. There is a waiting list so long for the apartments that you can be on it for 20 or 30 years. But I didn't accept this, so I fought the government legally to make them do what they promised to do, and after three years of a legal battle, I won. So now I have somewhere permanent to live, to make my home.

I am happy for now, in this moment.

When I was 18 I felt I needed to know something about my family and my parents because I knew nothing at all. I found the place where I was born and I went there, to have a look at it and to see if there was anyone I could talk to. When I got there, there was nothing left, the house had been burned down. But I did find a neighbour, an old man who had been there for a very long time, and I started to speak to him, asking what happened to the family who used to live here. He told me 'there was a lady who lived here. At first, she was working, a good woman, then she started drinking. She drank a lot and she had many different men coming to see her. She also had a baby.'

He didn't know that baby was me.

He carried on talking: 'She would leave the baby outside if it cried, even during the winter, in the snow. One evening, she was drinking with a man and they started to fight. She was badly beaten up and as a result, brain damaged.' Apparently I was about two at that time, but I don't remember anything at all. I was taken to hospital when she was taken away, and from the hospital I must have been sent to the orphanage.

Once I knew she was alive, I began to look for my mother. One of the TRWL volunteers helped me, Jean McCarthy, and eventually she found my mother, who was in a mental home in Bryansk; by then, she had been there for 15 years.

This volunteer came with me, and together we went and visited. I was really scared. I was thinking, 'you're going to visit your mother'. But what is a mother?' I knew that I was OK on my own, but I also knew that I needed to see her, to ask her some questions. I didn't expect anything from her, just maybe some answers. I didn't expect her to say anything like 'I'm sorry I left you. I'm sorry I didn't take care of you.'

In fact, it wasn't a good meeting. The mental hospital was a cold, miserable place. I started to talk to my mother, asking her what had happened, because I wanted to understand something about my past, but she couldn't tell me very much. She said, 'yes, I remember, I had a baby. But I also had another two babies, girls.' So it seems I have two sisters that I never knew about. My mother said my father was a good man, but he left with the other two children, my sisters. I have never been able to find him or them so I don't know what really happened.

My mother was shocked to see me. She was brain damaged, but she realised that something bad had happened to her that meant she could not look after the child. She was quiet, staring out the window. In the end, after all that time, my mother had nothing to say to me, we just sat and looked at each other in silence.

I visited her once more. I wanted to ask her the same questions, to see if her answers were the same or different. They were the same, such as they were, but she had very little to tell me.

She wanted me to take her out of the hospital, to come and live with me, with somebody from her own family. But I couldn't do that. It was too much. I didn't want to live with her.

All my life, I was used to living for myself, by myself. I was ok without her and didn't want to take responsibility for her now that she was old and sick. I had no bad feeling for her, but I was too used to living without other people. I wanted to see her, to try and understand the reasons why my life happened the way it did. But she couldn't explain anything, and after the second visit I didn't go again.

In fact, talking to the old neighbour, I understood more. He said I don't look like the man whose surname I have, that I look like a different man who used to come around to the house. He also said there was a grandfather living there with my mother and me. One day, I might try and find this grandfather and talk to him.

I'm sure that what I know is not the full story, even now. But I am ok without any family. I am proud of myself, proud of the people close to me who put their soul inside me and showed me the proper way to live. I don't drink, I don't smoke, I don't do bad things. I try to work, to get results, to live better. I have my own family now, my wife, and together we will make our own lives."

✳

Slava Lunicov (26).

Businessman

A challenging, sometimes difficult child when he was in the orphanage, but very intelligent and motivated. He got a place at the naval Academy, a very big deal for an orphan, but after two years there his behaviour was such that he was returned to Hortolova. This was humiliating and a set-back for him, but he succeeded despite everything. He graduated university and got a job as a lawyer but has now set up his own business, which is doing well. Married, with one daughter.

"When I come back to Hortolova, all my life flashes before me. The bad moments and the good moments. I was here from the age of 10, and before that I was in another orphanage from the age of three. It's difficult to think back because everything seems to have happened so quickly. Thinking now, it doesn't seem so hard to be moved from one orphanage to another, but at the time, I know it was hard to leave the first place and go somewhere else.

Why did I end up in an orphanage? I don't know. You would need to ask my mother, but she is dead. I had no contact with her from the time I was three, except for one meeting. She was in prison for years, and then I don't know where she was. She didn't ever come looking for me. I have a much older sister, who was in a different orphanage. She came to visit me once; she is 10 years older and was already settled in her life. I stayed with her for holidays a few times, but not often. She wasn't like a mother to me. She has two children of her own and we are not that close, although we are in touch.

Slava Lunicov: "When you are small, you adapt very quickly to any circumstances and so I got used to Hortolova."

I don't remember my father, I don't know anything about him. He died when I was one. The only time I remember meeting my mother was when I graduated from here. I was 18. I went to my sister's and I met her there. She just said 'hi' to me, and I said 'hi', and then 'bye'. I had no feelings for her, she was just like a stranger on the street to me. I didn't ask where she had been and she didn't tell me. After that, I didn't look for her or try to find out where she was.

Even when I say 'mother,' I don't feel anything, it's just a word to me. Maybe she tried looking for me, but if so, I am not aware of it. She had chances to find me if she really wanted to, and she didn't. My mother is dead now. She was in touch with my sister, but there were more arguments than communication. They lived together sometimes, on and off, never happily.

When my mother died, my sister and I became part-owners of a very small flat in Bryansk, and I signed my share over to her. She was married, she had children, she was already living there. I was single and I was determined to make my own way in the world. So I gave the flat to her. Since then we have been closer, but she has her family and I have mine, and we don't mix them too much. Maybe it's better like that.

When you are small, you adapt very quickly to any circumstances and so I got used to Hortolova. I came here before Debbie arrived and yes I remember the difference. Everyone does. Everything became much better for us. It's not just the money – yes, a lot of money was spent and buildings were rebuilt, but other things became different as well. Before Debbie, we were in Hortolova all the time, we never, ever saw anything except this place, these carers. We didn't know anything about the world, we didn't even know anything about the city close to us, just the woods, the other

Slava Lunicov with his daughter: "I wanted to stand on my own feet, to get away from the orphanage and make a new life for myself, so I got a job for the hours I wasn't studying, found a flat and paid the rent."

orphans and the buildings we slept, ate and studied in.

Once Debbie came, she started to bring new people – Trisha, Mairtin, Ciara, Larry, Dermot, John Patchell, Emma, Sophie, Louise, Lavinia, Lorna, Zhenya, Eamonn, Fiona, Kim, Ciara, endless Irish came. I cannot remember all the Irish there was so many, they brought many new things to us. We began to go out, to visit other places, go on excursions, visit cities in Russia that we read about like St Petersburg and Moscow. Doing this opened our eyes and our horizons. Debbie wanted us to see how beautiful Russia was. Most of only knew what a forest looked like.

For me, this was wonderful. I always knew I wanted something

"I believe that everybody has a determination to succeed, but not everyone is able to because of different circumstances holding them back. If you create the right surroundings for achievement, everyone will try. That's what Debbie did."

different to the others. As orphans, we had a set of professions available to us – brick-layers, panel beaters, plumbers, that kind of thing – but I wanted something that wasn't on that list. Something better. I always wanted to be outstanding, I didn't want to be in the group with everybody else.

I know very well that nothing like what happened for me, what became possible for me, would have been available if Debbie hadn't come here. No matter how outstanding I felt I could be, if I had been left to go the way leavers from Hortolova usually went, my life would have been just like theirs – low-paid, low-skilled jobs without any advancement or possibility. I think the frustration might have ruined me.

Thanks to some good orphanage staff, when I was about 13, I was accepted to a very good school, the Naval Academy in St.

Petersburg. It was a huge achievement to get in there, but I didn't make a success of it. Maybe I just couldn't cope with the fact that I was alone there? Maybe I felt too lonely, too isolated among all the family children? Maybe I was just afraid of being in a different place, of facing different life and different perspectives? Anyway, I couldn't adapt, I couldn't cope, so I misbehaved, I did very wrong things. I made no friends while I was there, I always felt excluded and isolated.

The level of discipline was much higher at the Naval Academy than Hortolova. In the orphanage, we had timetables and routines and discipline, but in fact, the carers weren't all that strict. There, the discipline was military, and very adult, from the very start. There was no concession to the fact that we were children. So I had to face this grown-up world very young, a world completely different to the one I had known, and it just didn't work for me. I was there for about two years, and I misbehaved almost constantly. In the end, they had enough, and they sent me back to Hortolova.

Once I got back to the orphanage, I regretted deeply what I had done. I felt humiliated by my failure, and the other boys who had perhaps thought I was arrogant before I left, were happy to see me fail. They used this as an excuse to tease me. Although I was well able to defend myself physically, I couldn't stop them taunting me. As I became more mature, I continued to regret that I had not succeeded.

The older I got, the more I realised that coming back to the orphanage was a step backwards in my life. I didn't realise immediately, but once I grew up a bit, I really knew it; that I had won a great opportunity for myself, but that I had failed to take it.

I tried not to let this destroy my confidence. I just tried to carry on. It was a good thing that Debbie was there to support me when I came back. Without her, it would have been even more difficult. She didn't judge me or let me believe that I had missed my one chance. Because of her, we orphans already knew that we could achieve more in our lives than ever before.

She had started the Leavers Programme by then with a really great Irish man called John Patchell, and through that we knew we had more options, more opportunities. That helped me very much. And I was determined that I would not fail a second time. I believe that everybody has a determination to succeed, but not everyone is able to because of different circumstances holding them back. If you create the right surroundings for achievement, everyone will try. That's what Debbie did.

Through the Leavers Programme I received extra grinds, I did my driving licence, and I was accepted to university in Bryansk. There too I had total support from To Russia With Love. At that stage there was no Life Skills Centre in Hortolova, so we didn't know anything at all about how to cook, how to use a washing machine, how to plan a week's food budget. So we had a survival camp before we finally left the orphanage; a week in Peter's Place in Bryansk, where we were taught how to cook, how to shop by Zhenya, who was working with Debbie and really good to us all, he still is to this day.

We were given an address of a place that we didn't know and we had to find our own way there, by asking for directions from people on the street. It might sound stupid, but we didn't know how to do any of these things. We didn't even know how to talk to someone in a shop and ask for what we wanted. In the evenings we watched movies, films about drugs, about alcohol abuse, and discussed them. Zhenya was a role model to us all.

We had one life in the orphanage, and we had to learn another one when we left there. You can't do everything in a week, and reality is of course very different to a lesson, but it was a start. That week prepared me for life, and gave me confidence. It was interesting.

Academically, I was well able for the course in university. Thanks to the life skills I learned, I could handle the social side as well. Soon I didn't want to live in Peter's Place anymore. I wanted to stand on my own feet, to get away from the orphanage and make a new life for myself, so I got a job for the hours I wasn't studying, found a flat and paid the rent. I made new friends in university, and I met my wife. Now we have a daughter together.

I still go back to Hortolova, I bring toys for the kids who are there, and help in whatever way I can. Actually, I think the children who are there now are a bit spoiled, compared with us. They get too many presents. We never had that much. We got presents, but we didn't get bikes or Playstations they way they do. I am afraid they will get used to good things very quickly, and they will expect the same after leaving.

When I finished university, I went to work for a bank, as their in-house lawyer. A year ago I was made redundant and with the money I received, I started my own business, which is going well. I am not satisfied yet, not by a very long way. This is only the beginning. There is no limit to growing, getting better, to achieving more and more, and I will not stop until I have achieved everything possible."

❊

The Children's Stories Part II

These are the children aged 15-18 who are preparing to leave Hortolova, either at 16 or at 18, depending on the academic year they leave in. Our staff wish that many of them could stay on longer, because they are still very helpless and need extra help and extra tuition.

Our children have many problems. Their cognitive abilities tend to be lower than family children of the same age, because of the terrible neglect in their childhoods. They long for tenderness and kindness, and react very badly to criticism. You want to mind them and be kind to them so much but staff also know they also have to instil discipline.

A lot of these children exaggerate the stories of their lives – by making

"Our children have so much routine – a routine that never varies, not on the holidays or at weekends – and that is hard for them."

159

the story better, brighter than it really is.

They will tell you everything was wonderful when they lived with mamma and papa, that their parents were kind to them, fed them, treated them well. They will say they have no idea why they were taken away from their homes. If their parents were raging alcoholics, they might say, 'well, they have a few drinks sometimes, but not so much...' They say it because they want it to be true. And because they have no point of comparison. They don't know what normal family life is like.

They usually seem much younger than their age. Our fourteen and fifteen-year-old girls still play with dolls. This is because they see so little of the outside world – they have no access to media really – but also because they have had no proper childhood, so they are not ready to leave it and become adults. They are too old for their age because they have seen too much violence and neglect, but then they are too young for their age in other, emotional ways.

Even the sixteen and seventeen-year-olds who have left the orphanage are very helpless. If they need to go to the doctor, one of our staff has to take them. They phone constantly, with little problems that they should be able to sort out themselves.

Our children have so much routine – a routine that never varies, not on the holidays or at weekends – and that is hard for them. Also, they have no space to themselves; they don't have their own rooms, they share, so they never get away from each other, and they are exhausted just from always being with each other. Some of them badly need space to get away from each other, so they find a corner somewhere and make it their own. If other children intrude on that little bit of private space, there can be furious arguments.

They want to get out into the world, but they don't know how to be when they get there; what to do, what kind of people to connect with and form relationships with. They've had such hard life experiences that they should be scraping to get the best of life, being ambitious and trying to get to the top, but unless we keep a careful eye on them, they tend to make the wrong friends who show them bad examples, because they keep recreating the bad relationships from their early lives.

We badly want to keep these children longer, monitor them closely once they are out in the world, because they are not ready, after years of dysfunctional families and institutional life, to make their own way in the world. We may not be able to keep them, but we will stay with them as they go on their journey.

※

Leonid (18).

Leonid is a gentle, thoughtful boy who speaks in a low voice. He has a stutter that he is gradually overcoming, and is still suffering trauma from the death of his mother when he was four. He leaves Hortolova this year, and hopes to train to be a mechanic.

"I don't regret being here. I was raised well and I have had opportunities that I wouldn't have had otherwise, and I have learned to be more disciplined about what I need to do. This year is my last, I have been here for six years. When I leave, I will go to industrial college, to learn to be a mechanic.

I came here when I was 12. It was a bit scary because it was unusual. I was all by myself, I didn't know anyone and there was no one to talk to, but I got used to it and made friends.

I was in a shelter home before I came here, for about six months. Before that, I was with my father and his civil wife. My brother is 28 and my sister is in her 30s, so I was the only one still living at home. My mother died in 2000, when I was four. It was on the 2nd of January, there was a fire in the house. Me, my father and my brother all got out in time, but my mother went into the kitchen for something, and she didn't get out in time. She died in the fire, while we stood outside.

Straight after, I was taken to the neighbour's house, I looked out the window and saw two figures standing there and a third, on the ground, under a cover. That was my mother but I didn't realize it. I asked my father when was my mother coming and he didn't answer, but his friend was there and he said 'soon'. I don't remember her, what she looks like. I only know her face from photographs. I have a lot of photographs.

That was the end for my family. My brother and sister had a different father, so they went to live with him, and I lived with my godparents while the rebuilding happened. Then, when it was finished, I lived with my father and my grandmother. My mother's death shattered my father, it swept him away, he started drinking a lot. Sometimes he drank before that, but not much and mostly he worked. Even when he was drinking he would go to work. The people he worked with would come and get him and take him to work, so he never got fired.

Then he had a new civil wife. She was nice and kind, but then she started to drink too. They were drinking together, and when they went into the black hole of drinking, she was different. I would move into my grandmother's room and stay with her, stay out of their way. The black hole would last two or three weeks sometimes, and then my father didn't work any more.

I would play the computer, skip school, no one minded me or cared for me. My grandmother would get me some things to eat, but she was afraid to go out too. There would be drama and fights between my father and his civil wife, and between the people who came to the flat. There were always people – they drank too. It was an open house, with bad people coming in and out, other alcoholics. Sometimes they would fight with me also and my father would shout at me.

I missed so much school that one day one of the staff at school said 'would you like to go to a shelter house, just to have a look? If you like it, you can stay, if you don't, you don't have to.' I was crying a lot and didn't want to go, but I did, and then they tricked

**Leonid's Story
The To Russia
With Love
View**

"When Leonid says that until his mother died, his life was fine, we don't know if that is true. It's what all the children say."

Leonid is clever and, if he decides that a mechanic is what he wants to be, he should be well able for the course. He knows how to create a bond with people around him, with the teachers and staff who can help him.

Leonid has a good attitude towards his father. He says that when he was not drinking, he was a good father. That's his view of things – it's the view of a child who wants things to be this way, but in reality, it wasn't like that at all from what we know of the case.

His father died recently. Leonid doesn't know what his father died of, only that there was a fight the night before he died. There were a lot of fights in that house, Leonid's father and his civil wife kept open house for anyone who cared to come.

We have some experience of the way they lived, because there was a boy here in Hortolova, Vanya, who left a couple of years ago and was enrolled in the technical college. Within two months he disappeared. We went looking for him and eventually tracked him down.

It turned out that Vanya was living with Leonid's dad, so we went there to look for him. The flat was in the city centre, a nice big flat that should have been a pleasant place to live, but the state of it inside was horrendous.

me into staying. I didn't want to stay but I found there was no way to get out. I was crying so much. My father came to see me that day, and then I calmed down a bit. He said he would take me home at the weekends. It was sad at first and I wanted to go home, but

There were minimal furnishings and everything was half-broken, torn wallpaper and carpets, people everywhere, some asleep, some awake, drinking. They were all alcoholics.

The smell was terrible and everything was filthy, ugly. So I saw myself where Leonid's dad was living. We didn't even walk in, it was too risky; we just looked in long enough to get Vanya back. We took him away, put him back in the technical college and had a big long talk with him.

So when Leonid says that until his mother died, his life was fine, we don't know if that is true. It's what all the children say.

Even if there were cases of alcoholism, they all say 'everything was wonderful, we had a great life until X, Y Z happened.' They say it because that's the way they want things to be.

There were two children here a while ago, girls, who told us they came from a very nice family, very wealthy with lots of property. That their mother died suddenly and their father was killed.

A nice foster family took them away straight away and now the children are finishing 10th and 11th grade. They are good in school and try hard. Recently, staff members, with social services, began looking into their circumstances, getting all their paper work together, looking into background of the family and trying to establish the children's rights to any property in the estate.

It turned out through the investigations that the mother had been drinking heavily from the age of 15 and died of alcohol-related disease at 25. The father was 15 years older than her and drank too; he got involved with the mafia and got killed. The girls have legal rights to a fraction of a

there were other children there and I got used to it. We didn't fight, we were like a little family, we looked after each other.

My father died in August last year. Before that, we saw each other, he would come and visit me sometimes. I don't know what studio flat, along with some other people, who don't want them to have any rights there and are prepared to fight it.

So the story turns out to be completely different to the one they told. This happens very often and we know to expect it. The way the children remember it, no matter how terrible their lives, when they lived with their parents, everything was wonderful and they had ice-cream every day.

But sometimes they will never have seen soup, never eaten it. Soup is a staple of all Russia diets, if they don't know what soup is, it means that no one was taking care of them at all. Buying a child an ice-cream one day because you are drunk and in a good mood is not the same as caring for them and feeding them properly, but for the child, all they know is they got an ice-cream. Leonid wants his story to be nice, but sadly it may not actually be.

he died of. The police didn't say, just that there was a fight and he died in the night, but they didn't exactly say what happened. When he was not drinking, he was a good father to me; he loved me. I miss him.

My grandmother used to come every weekend, but she died in 2008, on the day of my father's birthday. My sister said she wanted to take me to live with her, and I went to see her and stay with her for a few days – she is not married, but she has a child – but that was a few years ago, and I haven't seen her since then. Sometimes my brother and I call each other and see each other, but not very often.

Now that I am here in Hortolova, my life has more order, more focus. I have made up the school that I missed. It was hard, there was a lot I had to do, but I did it, and I got back up to the standard where I should be bit by bit. Also, I have gained more confidence and a better view of the world."

Irina (17).

Irina came to Hortolova when she was 11, and is soon to leave. She hopes to study to be a nurse or a paramedic. Tall, open and confident, she has always been very popular with staff and children, and staff believe she has a good chance of success in life.

"I came here three years ago this month. I was roaring crying for the first few days; I just wanted to go home. I was scared and lonely. Before coming here, I was in the shelter house for two or three months, and I thought I would go home from there. Instead I came here, and that was hard for me to accept. But after a few weeks it got easier, I made friends and I settled down.

My best friend was a girl called Vicka, who died last year. No one knew she was sick. She liked running, skiing, everything sporty. She participated in all the competitions and won medals. That evening, she was just walking along the corridor, and she collapsed. I was close by and I heard another girl screaming and calling to me, and I went to her. No one knew she had any problems, and then she just died. It has been very hard without her. Now I don't have close friends, just classmates. Being here without her is not the same.

I will leave this year. Then I hope I will go to study to be a nurse or a paramedic. That will be four more years of study but it is worth it for a good job.

Before the shelter home, my two sisters and I lived with our granny, who took us in after my father stabbed my mother when I

**Irina's Story
The To Russia
With Love
View**

"At the moment Irina wants to be a nurse, but she changes her mind a lot. Last month it was something else. It is very difficult for any of our children to answer the question."

Irina is very good and very polite. She lived with her grandmother until she was quite old, so in comparison with the other children here, she is like a family child. She is never rude to the carers, is a good all-rounder: she likes to draw and do embroidery, she is interested in sport and school. You can teach her anything, because she is interested and she wants to learn.

Irina has a large scar on her forehead from when she was really young. We don't know exactly what happened, possibly one of her grandmothers, after they started drinking, did something, maybe they dropped her or she got hit.

She is a capable person, and

was nine months old and my sister was a few years old. They were drinking, and then my mum died, and my father went to prison because of that. So my granny took us, my mum's mother. But she couldn't cope with the tragedy of losing her daughter, and after a few months she began to drink too. She couldn't mind us because she was drinking too much, so we went to the other granny, my father's mother, and we stayed there until I was 10.

Then my grandfather died. Soon after, my uncle died in a fire, and then my aunt died too. My grandmother lost her husband, her son and her daughter, one after another in a short space of time. She was a good woman, but couldn't stand so much, and she started to drink also and not to take care of me. Before my granny started drinking, she was a good granny, but after, we were persistent. She will stick at something and try to finish even if it is hard. Most of our children, if tasks are hard, they get discouraged and irritated. They have psychological problems and they don't cope well with frustration. We try and encourage them not to give up, to keep trying.

If we see them getting upset, we stop the task instantly, give them something easier and more fun, then come back to the hard task about half an hour later, and try to help them.

At the moment Irina wants to be a nurse, but she changes her mind a lot.

Last month it was something else. It is very difficult for any of our children to answer the question, 'what do you want to be?' because they have no role models, they don't really know what is possible. Also, what puts them off is the studies and how difficult these can be.

They don't cope with the curriculum and the responsibilities easily, so they tend to choose easy subjects. Also, our children typically have very low self-esteem, they don't believe they are capable of much and so they don't want to try.

neglected. We didn't have food to eat, we missed a lot of school. It is hard to make yourself go to school when you are young, even though you should. If no one says it, you don't go.

She got a few official warnings but nothing improved, so she was deprived of her guardianship. My sister had already left for the technical college by the time this happened, so I was on my own. I was taken from my grandmother, brought to a shelter house, and then to Hortolova. I did not wish to move, I thought I could take care of myself even if my granny wouldn't take care of me, but now that I am here I can see that it is a better place, and I can concentrate on my work at school. Once I settled down, I knew that it was better here. The staff are nice here. It is nice to be here, the Irish are so kind to us and the Russians that work for them are fantastic, they get us all the things we need. It is nice to have someone take care of me.

My father renounced his parental rights when he went to prison, so when he came out of prison, he never tried to find us or make contact and now nobody knows where he is. I don't think I will see him again. I don't know where to look for him, and I don't think he will ever try to find me. I have photos of my mum still, but no photos of my dad and I don't know what he looks like. I don't think I would recognise him if he came any day.

"Before my granny started drinking, she was a good granny, but after, we were neglected. We didn't have food to eat, we missed a lot of school."

Both my grandmothers are still alive, and both are still drinking. I don't communicate with either them, they don't come and visit me, they just spend all their money on alcohol. I hear that one of them is getting dementia – she drinks all the time, she doesn't eat and has nothing in the cupboards at home – so she is very sick. I would like to see how she is and be in touch with her, but it is hard if she will not make an effort for me.

My sister is in Bryansk, working as a chef, we are still very close. When I go to Bryansk to study first, I won't live with her because I have no money for rent so I will live in the hostel of the technical school, because that is free for orphans. But maybe afterwards, when I am finished there, we can live together. I would like that.

If I have a chance, after I study to be a nurse or a paramedic, I would like to think I will maybe go on to third level education and study to be a doctor. I would like to help other people if I can."

"Most of our children, if tasks are hard, they get discouraged and irritated. They have psychological problems and they don't cope well with frustration."

171

Yuri (15).

Yuri has a minor disability – two of the fingers on one hand are joined together – but he does not let this hold him back and plays keyboard very well. He also has TB but so far this has not developed into a full-blown infection.

"I have been in Hortolova for nearly five years. The first thing I remember noticing about being here was the playground with the swings and slides. Before Hortolova I lived in a shelter home for two years. I liked it, my family lived across the road, and they would come and visit me two or three times a week. My dad died when I was six and mum started to drink so I went to live with my aunty.

Then I was moved to another aunt's house and my mum never came to visit. My mum has two sisters who are younger than me, and they were being sent to a shelter home, so I decided to go with them, to try and make sure they weren't hurt or that anyone was mean to them. I chose to go, because it was the manly thing to do.

The shelter home was just across the fence from my aunt's house where I was living, so I didn't move too far. We were all there together at first, my mum's sisters and I, but then we got separated, and I went to a foster family for two years.

When I came back, they were gone. I know where they are. They aren't too far away from here, in a different orphanage, but I don't see them. I contact them sometimes through my aunt. They have my mobile number and when they can, they will call.

The foster family I went to lived not far from the shelter home. I

**Yuri's Story
The To Russia
With Love
View**

"Yuri is very tactile, affectionate and chatty. He can talk from dawn until dusk, to anyone who will listen."

From birth, Yyuri had a minor disability; two of the fingers on one hand were joined together, so essentially he has three fingers on one hand. Initially the government classified him as disabled, which gave him the right to extra social welfare payments, but since he turned nine the classification was revoked because he was deemed able and competent.

He plays keyboard well and the disability doesn't prevent him from doing this. He is a careful person, and keeps his things very close to him. He doesn't like to share too much, but he doesn't ruin or break his things, he keeps them carefully. Also, he only wants his own things. He doesn't ask for much, he is very modest in his requests.

Yyuri really loves his mother. In all the years that he has been here, he never stops hoping that she will come back for him, to take him away, or even to visit. After she left, he found her himself, with some help from us, but mostly through his aunts. She was living in Moscow.

He got her number and made contact through one of his aunts, his mother's sister. He still tries to get in touch through this aunt; but his mother doesn't respond in any way. She moves around a lot, no one seems to know where she is or is going to be, so it is difficult to maintain contact, and she has no desire to do so.

Yuri has TB and spends quite a lot of time going back and forth from hospital because he keeps testing positive. He is infected, but the disease hasn't multiplied yet, so he needs to be checked all the time to be sure it's not active. There is a good chance it will never become active; as long as he takes the pills for a few years, he should recover perfectly. When he is in hospital, he is there for three months at a time. We visit him, and we arrange for his aunt to phone when we are there so he can talk to her then. She also comes to see him here sometimes, and twice has tried to take him home to her house for a weekend or a short holiday, but she works and doesn't have much time. Yuri is very tactile, affectionate and chatty. He can talk from dawn until dusk, to anyone who will listen. He is not an aggressive or confrontational boy, and never shouts. He likes to read, a habit he picked up from hospital when he was there on his own for so long. No one has time to visit sick orphans in hospital so the To Russia With Love girls do this all the time.

was there for two years, and it was ok, but then I stopped living with them. I don't know why. I was surprised when they told me that I would be moving and I didn't want to go. They didn't tell me anything about why. The grandmother was old, maybe that was why?

My mother is in Moscow but she's still drunk. I phoned her once, but after that I stopped wanting to talk to her, because I was so hurt. Do you realise how much it hurts? One aunt comes to visit me, she took me to her house for the Spring holidays. My mum wants to come back, but she is in an institution that she cannot leave freely.

You can check yourself in, but you need a certificate from a doctor in order to get out. I don't even think about what I would do if she came back. I don't know if I would see her.

When I'm older I want to play keyboard, maybe with a band. I want to study in the institute in Bryansk, I am hoping the Debbie and the Irish will help me. and then I will go back to the town where I lived with my parents, where my family are."

Alla (17).

Soon to leave Hortolova, Alla wants to study agriculture. She is a cheerful, biddable girl, but may have an undiagnosed learning difficulty. Staff say she will need to focus far more on her studies if agriculture is to be possible. Alla's older sister, Vica, was in Hortolova for only a year, and since leaving has been leading a troubled lifestyle, which worries Alla.

"There are no good memories of being at home at all. It wasn't a good family. The only things I remember are bad things, because only bad things happened. I remember my father twisted my arm when he was drunk. I remember my grandmother lived with us and my father taught me to steal money from her. 'Get me money for a drink, and remember where she keeps it,' he told me. The money was from her pension and it was all she had. I remember people shouting, and drinking. My older brother lived with us for a time, but now he is in prison.

They didn't cook or feed us or take care of us. The neighbours would feed us sometimes, because all we had at home were potatoes, and only then if my grandmother made them. They would give us clothes too because they could see we didn't have any.

My older sister Vica and I were put in the shelter home when I was about five. What happened was that my father strangled himself on swings in the park one night, and my mother copied him a while later, but at home. I suppose she really, really loved him, and couldn't cope when he was gone. First she drank even

**Alla's Story
The To Russia
With Love
View**

"Alla doesn't take two steps ahead and think through her actions. She is impulsive and short-sighted."

We think that Alla might have a developmental delay, some kind of psychological difficulty, but it is not diagnosed. Alla and her sister Vica didn't get along. Alla tried, but Vica didn't understand that she needed to make an effort. Vica was here for just one year, she left in 9th grade.

She was diagnosed with a learning disability, and there are only a few places where such children can go to study after school. To Russia With Love placed her in one, and visited her every month, but it did little good. Vika drank, was uncontrollable in her behaviour, she did no studying – she didn't want to do anything, didn't want to learn. Vica is almost psychotic, she can throw things and get very aggressive. She doesn't make rational decisions.

Now she doesn't go to classes any more, instead she leads a chaotic and dysfunctional lifestyle. There is nothing we can do with her, except try and

more, and then she committed suicide too. The day my mother died, I remember Vica and my granny and I were outside the flat. My granny was yelling 'open the door!' 'open the door!' because it was locked, but no one opened. So we smashed a window and hurt ourselves on the glass, and my granny put us up to the window and we crawled through into the room, but it was too late, my mother was hanging from a rope and she was dead. Even though I was the youngest, very young, I remember climbing in that window with my sister. I was very scared.

Grandmother died soon after that, and we went to the shelter ensure that Alla doesn't go the same way when she leaves here.

Alla is very calm in personality, easy to establish a relationship with. She will show the side of herself that she thinks you want to see, and she is good at working out what that is. If she needs something from someone, she will get it. She doesn't even understand herself the processes she uses to get what she wants, but she is effective.

She has a boyfriend, who she met in the corrective classes at school. He too has a developmental delay, but he studies hard and he tries. Alla will not study. There's always something getting in the way, a thousand reasons why she can't: something hurts, she doesn't feel well, she doesn't have time.

Alla doesn't take two steps ahead and think through her actions. She is impulsive and short-sighted. She doesn't understand yet that she might not pass the exams she needs to study agriculture, which are difficult exams. Her cognitive abilities aren't as developed as they can seem when talking to you. She doesn't really want to try either.

At the moment, we are trying to say to her 'hold on about agriculture. Just pass your exams first, and then we'll see what the options are. Don't jump too far ahead.'

home. Then, for a time, Vica and I were in a foster family, for about five years, from when I was six. I never wanted to go to the foster family, but the director of the shelter home advised the family to take both of us. I held onto the railings and didn't want to go, but it was forced upon me.

I suppose the foster family were good people but they loved Vica more, and I didn't feel at home there and couldn't settle. It was a very strict family, especially the father, and when he drank, he drank for a week and was bad to us. Anything I did, I got into trouble for it, and Vica told tales on me. I was always the bad one, she was always the good one, even though now that she is grown up she doesn't lead a good lifestyle – she drinks and smokes and has contact with boys.

Eventually I ran away from that family, and Vica stayed. They didn't love me, I don't think they cared very much for me. I ran away, but I was brought back to them. Then, at school, I told the teacher that the foster father nearly got put into prison for bad things that he did, and the teacher called social services, so we were taken away from that family.

I came to Hortolova six years ago, when I was 11. I don't remember my first impression, I was crying a lot in those days, but I made friends quickly and I am happy here.

Vica and I were here for three years together, then she left when she turned 17. She was enrolled to study to be a chef, but she stopped studying and started not leading a good lifestyle. We talk sometimes but she is always asking for money, she doesn't have her own place or anywhere really to live.

Being in Hortolova I have learned not to lead a lifestyle like Vica's. Being here has helped with my schooling and education. I have a routine and I know when everything will happen.

Because of this, my attitude is better – the way I am with people, the way I go about trying to do things. These days, if I start something, I will finish it.

Studying and knowing that I know things has helped me to have more confidence, but I am still shy. Soon I will have to leave here, and I am very scared to do that. I would like to study in an academy - maybe agriculture? But at the moment I am just scared to leave. A new environment, new teachers, meeting new people and trying to form relationships with them. It is a scary idea for me. I love when Mairtin comes from Ireland. I would miss the Irish if they left, they are our friends. Olga and the staff here are so kind to us."

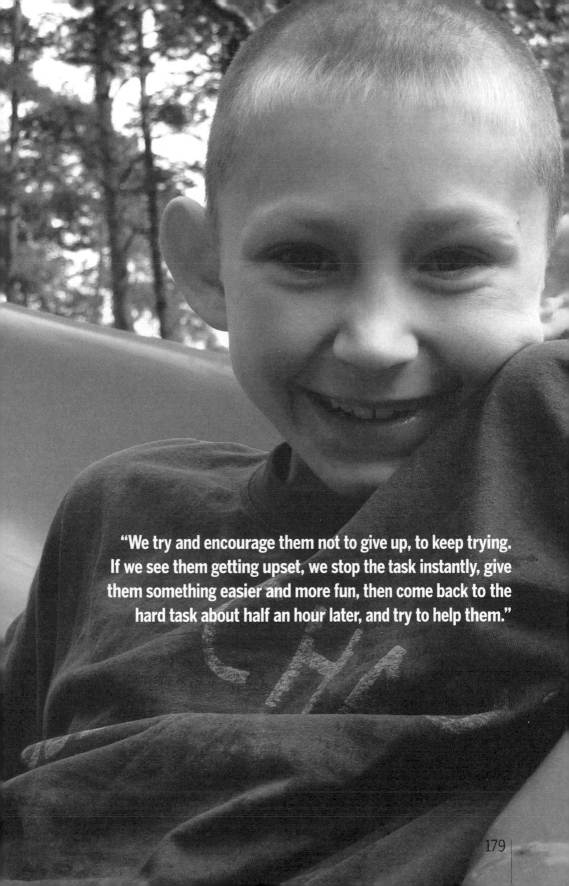

"We try and encourage them not to give up, to keep trying. If we see them getting upset, we stop the task instantly, give them something easier and more fun, then come back to the hard task about half an hour later, and try to help them."

179

Sash (16).

Sash will leave in September and plans to go to building college. He is a silent child who can have black rages. The scars left on his personality by what has happened to him are very strong, but staff say he is improving and is intelligent and capable.

"I have lived in this orphanage since I was seven, on and off. At the age of eight, I was taken by a foster family, where I stayed for three-and-a-half years. Things went bad for me there, I was a bit naughty, and so the foster family brought me back here when I was 12.

They were good to me in that family, they treated me like one of them and loved me. There was a boy two years older than me, and we became friends straight away. They never hit me, sometimes they shouted or maybe put me in the corner, but just like with their own child. It was my fault that everything went bad. I wasn't very good, I did bad things, and now I regret that. I didn't study, I fought, I was bad to them.

Every day the grandmother would collect us from school because my foster parents were working, but it was hard for her to handle me because she was getting old, so eventually the director of the school wrote a letter to social services saying the grandmother couldn't manage me. She was called for an interview with social services, who said she couldn't mind me anymore. So I was sent away. But their son stayed. I am still in touch with them though, and we have a good relationship. Still friends with the foster brother. We were really good friends, we're still in contact. When I go to visit the foster grandmother, I phone the brother and he comes and we see each other and it's really nice. They live in Bryansk.

I don't know anything about my father, I never met him or knew him. My mother and I had a flat near my grandmother. My mother would drink, with men who I didn't know. The men used to hit me. They beat me so badly that from the age of three I used to leave the house and just walk around the streets by myself to get away. The police would catch me and take me home, but the next day there would be more drinking, more men, and I would leave again. The third time this happened and the police found me, they took me to the shelter home instead of to my flat. I don't know if

"They beat me so badly that from the age of three I used to leave the house and just walk around the streets by myself to get away. The police would catch me and take me home, but the next day there would be more drinking, more men, and I would leave again."

they told my mum where I was, because she never came to see me.

I was there for a while, I don't know how long, then I was moved to another shelter home, and then I came here to Hortolova when I was seven.

I used to run away from the shelter homes. I didn't know the road or where I was going, I just used to walk and walk, and hope that I would begin to recognise something, that I would find my way home, back to my mother, but every time, the police found me. I thought eventually one day my mum would come and pick me up, even just visit me, but she never did. I haven't seen her since the day I left home at the age of three. I don't know where she is. I was given an address of where to go and look for her, and one day I went with my foster grandmother from the foster family, when I was 10, and there was only an old lady at the address who

**Sash's Story
The To Russia
With Love
View**

"So Sash terrorised the whole
village with his rages. He would
take the grandmother's pension
money and threaten her."

Sash suffered some kind of trauma to his eye when he was very young, something pierced it, like a pen or a bicycle spoke. He still has trouble with it, he is partially blind in that eye. He lived at home with his mother until he was three, which was not a good environment.

His mother had different men all the time, and some of them used to hit him, and his mother never stopped them.

Sash is a difficult child, but capable, as long as you explain to him specifically what you want from him and how he should do it. He has a problem with his aggression that has caused him great difficulty in the past.

He was taken by a foster family, but they brought him back when he was 14, and at first when he returned to the orphanage, it was terrible. He was impossible to talk to or influence in any positive way. He was aggressive – towards other children and the adult carers – unresponsive and unhappy.

His story still is that he was "a little bit naughty." In fact, he had major problems with aggression. In Russia, when people take children to foster them, they never look at the specifics of the child's story, their personality, or experiences.

They just pick them out of a line-up, usually because they are cute.

Then they don't understand how to be with such a child in a family environment, how to influence him in the right way, and the child doesn't know either, because almost always, these children have come from highly dysfunctional biological families, and they have never seen a normal family situation.

There is no training for the foster families, they just jump straight in and think everything will be lovely. Very often, it isn't. So Sash terrorised the whole village with his rages.

He would take the grandmother's pension money and threaten her. She collected him from school every day, while the foster parents worked, and she couldn't cope.

She was afraid of him.

Eventually she wrote a letter to social services asking that he be returned. Sash was told it was the director of the school who wrote, because the grandmother was scared to tell him that it was her who was sending him back, because she thought there would be serious consequences.

In the last year, Sash has been much better. He is a very different boy to when he came back first. He's had a big turnaround. He's older, he understands more about what went wrong in the family.

Also, he has a girlfriend now, for the past year, and he spends time with her and her family.

She is a very good influence on him. She holds him together and he is less aggressive.

It is good that he has this close relationship, because he doesn't have a particular friend in the orphanage, and no key adult that he has bonded with.

I would say the girlfriend is mostly responsible for his better attitude, but not entirely. Something clicked for him, a switch in his head that has shown him a different perspective.

He is still in contact with the son of the foster family. He goes to visit them, they take him for weekends sometimes and the relationship is friendly.

They can see he is a lot better than he was, but they wont take him back – he'll be 18 in two years time, there is no point – but at least the relationship is good.

We wish that Sash could stay longer with us. He is far from ready to face the world."

said, 'no, this woman left a long time ago.' So we have no idea where she is. Eventually, I accepted the fact that she wasn't going to come, that I was on my own.

There were about 10 people transferred from the shelter to Hortolova at the same time, all of us the same age. It was summertime, there were swings and slides here, lots of children running about. I thought – this might be interesting. I made friends easily with the other children and played with them. I like school here, I really enjoy history, algebra and general knowledge. I like football, and to walk in the woods. I try hard at my lessons. If I don't know something, I go and ask the teacher. Hortolova has been a good place to grow up. I was sad at first to come back from the foster family, but I have good friends here – my best friends are Pasha, Andrei, Ruslan and Leonid.

When I leave here, I would like to study construction – my interest in building comes from seeing one of the teachers who lives close to here rebuild his house. I watched him and then he let me help him, and I realised this is something I would like to study very much. I understand so many more things now than when I was younger, but I'm very scared to think of being by myself in the big wide world.

I'm going to try and find my mother when I am old enough. I don't have any aunts, uncles, grandparents that I know of, so I don't know how to start looking for her. The Irish might help me. But I will try to find her. I want to see where she is, how she's living, what she's been doing all these years. Everything is possible, it must be possible to find her somewhere."

"Our children long for tenderness and kindness, and react very badly to criticism. You want to mind them and be kind to them so much but, staff also know they also have to instil discipline."

Vanya (17).

A serious, thoughtful boy who makes great efforts to communicate and tell his story. Staff spotted that he is very intelligent, and arranged for him to go to the Lycium, a highly academic and prestigious school which ensures him excellent opportunities once he graduates. He found it almost impossibly difficult at first and probably would not have stayed except that he met a girl, now his girlfriend.

"I don't know if I can call my family a good one. My parents got divorced when I was very young. My mother and I lived very modestly, with my grandmother and sometimes my grandfather, because the financial position wasn't the best. My mother and my grandmother were both mentally ill, and there were many disagreements, sometimes between the three of us, but more often they argued between themselves and I stayed out of it.

I went to school, like any child, until one day when I was 11 my mother stopped letting me go. I don't know why. I would ask, 'can I go to school?' and she would say, 'No Vanya, you need to have a rest.' About two months after all this started, there were more and more disagreements, and more violent disagreements between my mother and grandmother.

They had more serious arguments and fights that got really bad. One day, two men came, I don't know where from, and they took my mother away. They left me behind, I stayed living with my grandmother and everything was quiet for about a week, and then different people came and took me to the shelter home.

I found it very hard to get used to that. There were many tears, I didn't want to be there. I wanted to be at home, I missed my mother and didn't know where she was. I worried about her. Bit by bit, I got into a routine. Every day was the same, no difference between them, and that was hard to get used to. I didn't have friends there. At first, because I didn't know anyone, but even when I did, they weren't friends.

There were a lot of fights, nasty ones, and maybe I was a bit fragile because women raised me, but I found it very difficult to see these fights and be part of them. I was there for two years, and it was always like that, it never got better. Two years is a long time to live in a shelter home, most people only stay six months. I don't know why I was there for so long. It was like a hostel, there is no one to help do your homework, no one to take care of you, no anything.

Sometimes my grandmother came to visit me. My mother found out I was living there and she was very sad, but she couldn't take me to live with her because she wasn't well enough. She would come every day to the shelter home, bring food and school things for me. Sometimes my grandfather came too, but not often, he was working and had too much to do.

After two years had gone by, a car came, a big Russian car, and brought me here to Hortolova. I didn't find that change so hard to get used to, because I had two years' experience of institutions by then, and this was immediately a much better place than the shelter home. The atmosphere was much nicer, I started to make friends, good friends; I was happy. There were trips away, like to a place in town where you can make cars and drive them. I liked that.

My mother didn't know where I was at first because no one told her, but then went I went home to see her, so now she knows. The government have given her a place to live, but she doesn't come to see me here. It is too far for her. I see her very rarely, she has TB and I'm scared to be too close to her in case I get it. Also, when I see her, she tries to control me. I don't like that. It isn't aggressive, it isn't total control, but I still don't like it. And my grandmother is 30km away, in a different direction, so it's hard to see them both.

My father is still alive, he lives in a town a bit closer than my mother and grandmother, but he has a big problem with alcohol. I don't see him, there is no contact between us at all. I saw him twice when I was little, about eight years old, and nothing since then. Any information I have about him comes from my grandmother

When I started school in Hortolova I did very well and the staff from To Russia With Love noticed that so I got extra help with study. I was always an A grade student, so when I was 12, I was offered to be a naval cadet. I was too scared to go there – it would have meant moving far away, again, and I was not ready for another move. Also, it is very tough there.

But, I would have gone, except that the Lycium was offered to me, a very good school and not so far away. I felt I could still be in contact with the staff from To Russia With Love there, and I could still call them if I had any problems.

I was an A grade here, but once I went to the Lycium, I was getting Cs and Ds. Everything was difficult.

No one really prepared me for how hard it would be, although they tried. I wanted to leave after the 8th grade, when I was 13, but I am an indecisive person, I couldn't make up my mind. Maybe that's a good thing? In the end, some of the girls convinced me to stay. After that, I worked harder, and in half a year I went from six Cs to just two. At 9th grade, when I was 15, everything became more stable, I started to get As and Bs again. I'm glad now I stayed. At the end of 9th Grade, I started a relationship with a girl I am still with, from Bryansk, who is in the same class as me.

During the summers I work in a friend's tile factory, and I play music. I taught myself the bass guitar bit by bit, because there weren't any teachers to show me. I also play accordion and acoustic guitar. For a while I played with a band with some guys from school. We had lots of rehearsals and we played a few gigs, a few festivals. We didn't get any better as a group, but it was fun.

But my girlfriend and I started to argue over the band – there wasn't enough time for everything, so I left the band and since then I have just been singing in a choir. The singing teacher said I had perfect pitch. They were surprised, it's very rare to have someone like that. So now I help to tune all the musical instruments and make sure they are perfect.

"I need to do better than other people, because I have fewer chances in life."

If I do well in my final exams at the Lycium, I can go to any university without having to sit the entrance exams, and I can study anything I want. I really like IT, music, general knowledge and English. I will definitely go to university – I've been working for this all my life. I need to do well, to do the best I can. I need to do better than other people, because I have fewer chances in life.

If I had stayed in the shelter home, or with my mother, none of this would have been possible. In that case, I would have stayed in the local school where I would have been prepared a little bit but not much. Life has been difficult, and moving so much was traumatic, but there will be good things from the hard times. To Russia With Love believed in me, that is why I was moved to a better school. They are very good people, they care about us."

**Vanya's Story
The To Russia
With Love
View**

"In the end, the love of his girlfriend changed him, not us...they are planning to go to Moscow University together."

Vanya is very focussed and disciplined now, but he wasn't always. He was very closed when he came first. He didn't talk, he wasn't sociable; he didn't express himself well so that made him shy of talking.

His mother has mental health problems and there were many difficulties at home with her and the grandmother. Then Vanya was two years in the shelter home, which is an unusually long time – I presume there were problems with his paperwork – and he was quite frightened there.

So when he came here, he was very quiet and shy at first. It took a few months to discover that he was bright, but when we realised, we decided to give him a chance and put him in the Lycium.

The first two years there were very difficult. It is a tough school. There are seven or eight lessons a day, four or five hours of homework every evening, and the rules are very strict. He wasn't ready for any of that.

The school was especially set up for bright children from the entire region, so some children come from up to 200 miles away. Because of this, there is a very good hostel attached to the school, where the children can live. There they get five meals a day, internet access, library, all looked after by carers day and night. It's basically like a very smart boarding school, and the children who go there are generally very well prepared for the high standard of education.

Vanya would never admit how much he was struggling and in trouble. Ask him how he was, and his response was always 'I am still alive'.

In fact, he was nearly sacked from the school because his marks were bad, he didn't study or do his homework, and his grades continually went down. Luckily, he has a very good class teacher, who from the start was interested in his success. She went to the director of the school nd pleaded his case. She also cheered im up from his bad moods, his problems nd troubles, and helped him with extra rinds.

When he is down, she phones me and ells me, then I know I need to visit him nd see how he is getting on. Some of our hildren are happy to see us when we visit nem. Others aren't – they are embar- assed, or pretending to be more ndependent than they are – but Vanya is appy.

At the same time as his class teacher ntervened, Vanya met a girl, and these two actors together have produced a very ood result. The girl is a really good influ- nce on him, the best. He has completely hanged since he met her. Now he is inter- sted in studying, doing his own work, and nusic.

It is always very slow to help a child like anya. We talked with him, worked with im, but you can't take a child with a errible story and expect them to be ealed within five minutes. In the end, the ve of his girlfriend changed him, not us.

He organised a band in the school and rote a song for her that he performed at ne school concert. All the girls in the class were crying because it was so romantic.

He is completely in love with her. They are planning to go to Moscow University together, and because of the change in his attitude, his marks will be good enough.

He is doing very well now. However, her parents are not very happy about the idea of them going off to Moscow together and living in a university hostel alone, so we will have to cross that bridge when we get to it.

If Vanya does go to Moscow, we can still take care of him. We have friends there, supporters and donors to TRWL, who will look out for him.

I cannot say for sure that Vanya will continue to study well and finish univeristy, but I hope he will.

He is able to do this, but it will depend on the people around him and the kind of influence they are. Our children especially are very dependent on the people around them, and very easily influenced for good and ill.

These children are all used to having the full To Russia With Love programmes, as they were not here before the Irish came. They think it is normal to be so well looked after.

Going the extra mile
By Patricia McGrath

Patricia joined To Russia With Love on day one. Trained as a nurse, she was one of the school gate mums who made up the original board of the charity. She has been on nearly every trip to Russia with Debbie.

My name is Debbie Deegan",are words that have defined my journey over the last 16 years. When the sentence begins "my name is Debbie Deegan…" it usually represents yet another chapter of the journey that has been my life since 1998, when a chance meeting at the school gate spun my world in so many pivotal directions that it would take another book to describe all it encompassed.

Debbie attracts attention and much recognition. She does media well, photographs look amazing with minimal touch-ups, column inches are easily filled and her many Russian medals would fill two

"My name is Debbie Deegan" must be the greatest addiction or affliction – I'm not sure which – that anyone could endure."

of Sylvester's chests – all well-earned for the many big things she has accomplished

But I am probably the only person privileged to have witnessed many of the 'real' charity moments, the little things that go unnoticed, are quickly forgotten, leave no photographic evidence, but yet have touched the lives of many and really do make a difference.

"My name is Debbie Deegan. I don't do discipline, I don't do rules and regulations. I don't suffer fools lightly. I am master at not accepting 'no' for an answer; in fact 'no' is the catalyst for getting the most out of someone or a situation." These traits should be listed on Debbie's calling card as a public warning. The flip side (and what I admire most) should read "kind, thoughtful, selfless, and belligerent if it means achieving something that will help someone else's plight."

Moments without cameras, journalists, celebrities; real life moments where there was nothing in particular to be gained, just the practice of true humanity. Going the last mile, as I have done so often with Debbie, is what keeps the addiction alight.

Driving an eight-hour round trip in snowy Russia just because she promised a child in Staradoop that she would come back to see him before Christmas. Hauling flower bulbs from Clontarf to Bryansk for a babushka she met along the road and whose tiny garden she thought would look nicer with crocuses. Buying the cow for the poor family with eight children so they could have milk daily. A special touch, hug or kiss that made so many children – adults too – along the way feel special.

So many times I have sat on the bus waiting to leave the orphanage after a long day while Debbie continued fighting with the authorities over the colour of paint or budget lines. So many times I vowed never to return, and yet…

"My name is Debbie Deegan" must be the greatest addiction or affliction – I'm not sure which – that anyone could endure. I have changed career, I have resigned as a director of the charity, I have tried to avoid contact with the powerhouse that is Debbie Deegan.

Frankly, escaping Alcatraz would be simpler.

We have done Russia together a hundred times. We did Romania and Beslan too, and what keeps me attached to the To Russia With Love web are all the many unforgettable moments.

This last week, it was sending one of our leavers to Moscow to see why she can't get pregnant, because Debbie wasn't satisfied with the test results in Bryansk, and so went that extra mile to help this now grown woman.

Last week in Clifden, Connemara we met a man who was alone and lonely, had turned 50 the previous day and had no one to celebrate it with. He was not long out of hospital having suffered extensive burns. Having an idea of where he lived, we eventually found his house in Dog's Bay, armed with a cake and candles. I wish the rest of the world could have seen that man's face. I don't believe he ever will be the same again.

Just because someone went the extra mile.

✳

The hope I found
Emily Hourican

Emily Hourican is an author and journalist who writes for the Sunday Independent. She has contributed to Condé Nast Traveller, Image Magazine, Woman and Home Magazine and Time Out, and published her first book, How To Really Be A Mother in 2013. She previously collaborated with Debbie Deegan on To Russia With Love, published in 2012.

Before my trip to Russia, I asked Debbie what I should bring over, what presents would the children like. 'Don't bring anything fancy or expensive,' she said. 'Our children aren't used to that.' So I brought a suitcase full of Chelsea football shirts that my eldest son kindly parted with. I hoped the kids in Hortolova wouldn't notice that they weren't this season's strip. They didn't, they seemed to like them, popping little blond and brown heads round the door of whatever room I was in, asking 'I want to tell my story. Can I have a Chelsea shirt?'

Later, in the Life Skills centre, where the children had made pancakes for the Irish Ambassador, visiting from Moscow, I found myself sitting surrounded by small boys wearing Chelsea shirts. I had spent the morning listening to their stories – the stories you have read here; terrible, tragic, depressing stories, any one of which would make national headlines in Ireland, and probably lead to questions being asked at government level about the provision of social services. In Russia, these stories, these children, are just a tiny handful among hundreds of thousands.

I had spent the morning efficiently putting my emotions on hold in order to gather the material I needed to help Debbie put together a book that would – we desperately hoped – raise money to continue the work that would help these children make lives for themselves out of the shattered debris of their childhoods. Really, there was no time to go to pieces.

But when I found myself surrounded by boys the same age and build as my son, wearing t-shirts that had been his, that I was so used to seeing him in, the full extent of the contrast between his life, the life of any child I can think of in Ireland, and theirs, was just too much. I began to weep steadily into my pancakes.

But I know the rules, Debbie has laid them out very clearly over the years, for me and for everyone else who makes this journey. We do not cry in front of the children, ever. We are not there to make them feel sad, but to cheer them up. We do not give in to self-indulgent sniffing, not for as long as they can see us. We smile, we laugh, we play with them, chat to them, hug them. Their need for physical affection is overwhelming – even the biggest ones will stand close, reach out and stroke your arm, lean in for a hug. Later, if we need to, we can sob until our hearts break, when the children are not there to see us.

I looked up to find Debbie and the lovely Irish volunteers giving me sympathetic but warning looks: 'We know how you feel. Now pull yourself together. For their sakes.'

What broke me was the feeling of hopelessness. All morning, the stories had kept coming, each one more pathetic and tragic than the last. So many crucial years in these children's lives had passed without kindness, care, attention. No one to read them stories again and again, stroke their hair, hold their hands, kiss them, hug them, laugh with them. Until they reach Hortolova, each one washed up in their own uniquely tragic yet shockingly familiar way, these little ones have known the worst side of humanity, and almost nothing of the love and attention our children take for granted.

The books on childcare that I have been addicted to ever since my first child was born all stress the supreme importance of the first two years. How the brain is formed by the interactions of these early years, how the patterns and pathways are laid down then that will last a lifetime, governing relationships, responses and reactions. How much effort we mothers must put in, in those early years to get it right, grow our children into happy, confident adults.

What hope had these kids, I wondered? For all the love and kindness that To Russia With Love puts into helping them, what chance do they have of ever making up the lost years? It was the sense of utter hopelessness that made me cry. The feeling I had that these years in Hortolova might be the only happy interval in lives book-ended by misery. That once out from the warm embrace of this place where the Irish have intervened so thoroughly, bringing our way of doing things into a uniquely Russian spot, the miserable patterns laid down by their early years would simply continue.

That evening I met some of the older orphans, the 26 and 27

year olds who are grown up now, out in the world, working, succeeding, making friends, setting up families of their own. And everything came right. They were so funny, so smart, so confident and articulate. So proud of themselves, in the best possible way. Beautiful – boys and girls alike – witty, well-turned out and so able for it all. They would have stood out in any crowd of young people I have met. Best of all, the girls who had brought their own babies along were calm and happy mothers, to children who were robust, laughing evidence that the cycle has been broken.

They are the hope we all need.

✳

The Children's Stories Part III

Our youngest children, aged 9-13, can be the hardest to fathom. Their stories are confused, contradictory, they don't follow logical sequences of time or place, and it can be difficult to make out what actually happened, as opposed to what they have told themselves happened. They are sometimes confused between foster families and biological families, and where they have had two foster families, the confusion is complete. There are more questions than answers in these stories – often just why?

Their stories are repetitive and sometimes rambling, but the cumulative effect of them taken all together, gives a complete picture – of the lives of children who have been neglected or

Some of the younger boys preparing for a concert.

abandoned by their families, who have been shunted around various institutions and alternative care; of the hardships of life in Russia, the endless bureaucracy that makes life impossible for orphans. And in the background are the tragedies of their parents: their incapacity, their failures, their hopeless addictions.

What is horribly clear is that these children have been failed, and failed again. By their parents, first, then by the wider family, and by the system, which cares for them physically, but doesn't put their welfare first and centre.

What shines through is their lack of sophistication – they have never heard of Man Utd, Chelsea, Disneyland. Their touching faith, the childish attempts they have made to hold their families together, the hope they still have that someone will one day come for them. The pride they have in the few family photos they might have, a man standing against a garden gate – 'Papa' – a woman against a tree – 'Mama'. These are all the connection they have with normal family life.

You never knew the word 'Mama' could be so sad, until you hear it uttered by these children, some of who can't remember an actual person, but still cling hard to the idea.

Andrey (10).

An adorable, blue-eyed, blonde boy; beautiful but with a closed, wary face. He doesn't make eye-contact and speaks in short, simple sentences.

"I speak a tiny bit of English. I can say 'my name is Andrey, I am 10.' I learned English in school here. I also learn drawing and playing football. This is my second year. I like it here.

Before, I lived in Bryansk city, with granny, daddy and granddad. My mother left to a different town, I don't remember when because I was too small. She never came back to visit. I liked living with my father and granny. It is better to live at home. I can ride a bike there, there were more places to walk around and visit. Here, I can only go in the orphanage.

I call my granny often and she comes every Saturday. Papa doesn't visit, but when I went home for Christmas he was there and I saw him. When I call my granny, I never speak to my dad. He is at work and when he comes home at 9 o'clock, he drinks and he doesn't want to talk. But he is a good dad, I love him, and he loves me.

No one told me why they took me away. I was at school and they just came and told me I had to go to the shelter house. I didn't want to go, I was scared, but I didn't ask any questions. I did what they told me. I spent two months in the shelter house, and they didn't tell me where I was going. My granny came to visit me, but only her. When I came here, Marina my carer met me, she is very good. Then Sasha and Roma, older guys, showed me around. I didn't like it at first. I was lonely but now I have friends.

When papa drank, sometimes he was very bad, sometimes he was ok. He didn't drink every day. Some days when he was drunk, he just went to bed. But some days he had fights with my granny, sometimes with granddad as well, quite severe fights. I heard him fighting with granny and I wanted to call the police, so they would come and stop it. But I didn't know how to so I went to my neighbours and they called. The neighbours took care of me a bit.

At home I have a room with my bed and a big plant and a carpet, and my toys. My favourite toy is my teddy bear, I don't remember the colour of the carpet, probably brown. My dad shares my room with me.

"I heard him fighting with granny and I wanted to call the police, so they would come and stop it"

My granny did the cooking, but when she was busy or sleeping, I cooked fried eggs for myself. I taught myself, I watched her doing it and I learned myself. My favourite food is dumplings. With my granddad, we would go fishing together – summer fishing, not winter. With my grandma, we went shopping. With my dad I went fishing as well. I caught the biggest fish, and I gave it to our cat.

My birthday was in March, and we went to the forest with the carers and we had a bonfire and we cooked potato and bread and had a celebration. I got presents – a cup and some Lego. At home for my birthday my granddad gave me a railway station and my granny made a cake. Last year at Christmastime I went home, and we went skating and skiing. I stayed for two weeks. This year I didn't go, my granny made the request and did the paperwork, but they wouldn't let me.

I dream of going back home. I don't know what can happen so that I can go."

**Andrey's Story
The To Russia
With Love
View**

"His father has become more violent and it is not safe for Andrey to visit."

Andrey is a very active, talented and artistic boy. He likes challenging, creative tasks, such as making something from nothing, and he is very patient and quiet. He can sit down to a 1000-piece puzzle and work his way carefully through it. When he came first, he was tense and not very communicative, but he has opened up more recently. In school, he has started doing better intellectually. He is learning well, and is intelligent. He is very good at reciting poems, very dramatic and professional.

He is a tender and affectionate child who likes hugs. He is open and trusting and well liked among the other children.

He is lucky with his grandmother who visits regularly, buys sweets for him and stays in contact. Sometimes she takes him home for holidays. He is very unusual among our children to have so many visits. His granny does what she can, but there is a limit to what she can do for Andrey while his father is still living in the flat with her.

He didn't go home this Christmas as usual because conditions in the flat have deteriorated.

His father has become more violent and it is not safe for Andrey to visit.

If the family ask for a child to be released for a visit, social workers will check carefully the circumstances of the home at that time, and if they are not suitable, the visit will be refused.

This is always devastating for the child, but we have to put their safety first.

Danya (9).

Withdrawn and quiet, Danya twists his hands together and is clearly uneasy being asked questions.

"Why are the Irish only here for a few days? Why do they not come back more often? It's good here when they come. Usually, it's ok living here; normal. Before here, I lived at home; I'm going home again for the long holidays.

At home are my sister, grandma and a cat, a big white Persian cat. My cousin is there too. And my parents are at home. Everyone is there except my brother, he died. He was 14. He fell from the ninth floor. I don't remember what it was like when I lived at home.

My mum was leaving, going to live in the village, and she said she would take me with her when I am seven, but I ran away and cried and said I wanted to stay where I was. I didn't want to go because it's boring in the village, it's more fun at home. There's no network in the village.

There was a big fight one day, with my cousin and my aunt, the grown ups. My cousin was sent to prison because he cut a hole in my aunty's side and she had to go to hospital. She's ok now, but she has a big scar. It was not my fault, but they were all in the other room fighting, the police came, they took me to the shelter home and then I came here. I liked it here at first, but then I did some things wrong and I got into trouble.

My favourite foods are bread and porridge, the people's food."

**Danya's Story
The To Russia
With Love
View**

"When he's happy, you can see it, he has very readable emotions, but a few minutes later can be completely different."

Danya is a very emotional child, and his emotional state changes constantly. He's smiling one minute, crying the next. Every small thing upsets him, he cries every day, many times. Even things like waiting to take his turn to read, he will insist 'I want to go first!' And if he can't, he gets upset and cries and goes into a rage. If he sees the other kids with something, he wants it, and thinks they should give it to him.

He needs his own space badly, and will go into the playhouse in the playroom and cover it with the blanket, just to get away from everyone. He's been here about a year and doesn't manage his emotions any better now than when he arrived; he's still just as explosive and voluble.

Time in the little playhouse helps him calm down a little, but otherwise he can explode and be very aggressive.

He makes stuff up, about himself, and other people. Any story he tells will be completely different to what actually happened. This comes very naturally to him; he doesn't actually know its not the truth when he says it, he believes it at the time.

All the boys are friends with each other, so the others don't like or dislike him, he's simply one of them. They might fight, but then they are friends again. Danya is active, involved in everything, but he can't concentrate for very long. He likes one thing one day, another the next. Mostly he makes it up as he goes along and doesn't stick at anything.

When he's happy, you can see it, he has very readable emotions, but a few minutes later can be completely different.

Like many of our children, he has sleeping problems. Never eating problems – they eat what they are given – but many of them roll themselves into their duvets at night and rock violently until they get themselves to sleep, they rock so hard the beds creak wildly. We do not have the right psychologists for these childrens' problems. Most of their problems are just broken hearts.

'If he's in a good mood, he'll make stuff up for you. If he isn't, you'll know about it."

But Danya is an appealing child who craves affection, he doesn't push you away, he always wants and needs attention. The attention has to be very specific – take him by the hand, take him with you places so that he is next to you all the time.

He likes physical contact, but he doesn't understand that people can be busy and not have time for him. He thinks that you have to pay him attention the second he wants it, and if you don't, he gets very aggressive and upset.

His aunts come to visit sometimes and take him for the holidays. He never mentions his mother or father, but from the information we have, all his family are alcoholics – grandma, grandfather, mum, dad – everybody is alive and everybody drinks.

Except for his older brother, who was in a different orphanage, and he died, either by falling or jumping, they aren't sure, from the 9th floor. What happened exactly is not clear; if he fell it's a tragedy, but if he jumped, it's a suicide, and no orphanage wants to take on that responsibility.

Danya thinks he will be fostered, but staff don't, because he is difficult, with psychological problems. If anything goes against him, or happens that he doesn't like, he can react very badly. He closes off so that no one can get through to him at all. He shouts and screams and lies on the floor. Because of his unbalanced state, he is unlikely to get into a foster family.

To look at, he's nice and smiley and talkative. He can be very relaxed and fun at times, but his psyche – he's extremely lazy, at everything, he doesn't want to study, to do his chores, to play sport. You need to tell him 1000 times, and give him 1000 reasons why he needs to do something.

"You never knew the word 'Mama' could be so sad, until you hear it uttered by these children, some of who can't remember an actual person, but still cling hard to the idea."

Sasha (12).

A sweet, affectionate girl, eager to please and very likeable. Shy and young-seeming, but with a cheerful sense of humour and infectious smile. (Brown Bag Films filmed Sasha over months to be their "Anya")

"I like Debbie and Mairtin and the Irish, and the teachers in Hortolova, everything is good here. I have good friends, I like school very much, all the lessons. I would like to be a teacher when I grow up. I have lived here for about three years. At first I didn't like it, but I got used to it. We have cooking classes on Wednesdays, we learn how to make potatoes, pasta, toast. We learn beading and embroidery too.

I was in a shelter home before Hortolova, for about a year. Before that I was with my family. First my parents were drinking, then the official people came and they took me to the shelter home. I don't know why I was taken away. Probably because my parents drank and left me on my own for a long time, but I was young, so I don't really remember. I do remember that my mother made good fried potatoes. I thought my parents took care of me well.

I have an 18-year-old brother; he came to the shelter home with me but not for long, and then he was old enough and he left. I didn't like it there. The beds were uncomfortable and lumpy, the walls were all rough and raggedy, it wasn't a pretty place. A few of the boys were nice, but most of them were not, and I was glad my brother was there to mind me.

There were grown ups there, but they didn't pay the kids much attention, they just brought them in and left them to their own things.

I was sad to leave my home. My parents don't come very often to visit me, but they did come once or twice to the shelter home. They live in a town four or five hours away from Bryansk. My brother lives in the same town as them and we speak on the phone sometimes, but he doesn't visit.

At first I thought the children here in Hortolova were strange, and that they would be mean too, but then I got to know them and I saw that they are kind. I needed to get used to the grown ups here too, I was scared of them at first.

This year I was invited to Ireland, I loved the family I stayed with, they were so kind to me, I hope I will see them all again. I want Ann Marie to be my Mama."

**Sasha's Story
The To Russia
With Love
View**

"She wants to forget everything that was in her past."

Sasha seems happy on the outside, but inside things are bubbling. She wants to forget everything that was in her past, so she won't talk about it. She lives in the present and doesn't tell anyone about what happened to her.

She is a sweet-natured, positive, active girl who has a lot of friends. Until "Anya" (the Brown Bag film), she didn't stick out from the crowd much, but now she has more confidence. She does embroidery very neatly and is capable of sitting for long spells and concentrating on one thing. She is good at school and good at sport. If you ask her to do something, she can do it, but you need to check it and make sure she did.

She's good with the younger children and might be able for a job working with children if she gets through technical college.

Kolya (13).

A quite, sweet, thoughtful boy with an appealing face. Kolya seems much younger than his 13 years. He is clearly immature and shows signs of wariness, but throughout the interview he tries hard to please.

"This is my third year here. I came from a village about 40 minutes by car from here, where I lived with my foster family. It was the neighbours who brought me here, because my foster family didn't have a car.

I knew Hortolova was a good place, because the foster family told me a lot of things about this place, good things, about everything I would do here. When I came it was April and all the trees were green and the flowers were blossoming and it was so beautiful, so I liked it straight away. It was difficult when I came here first, especially to make new friends, but here people help me with my homework, and I like the school.

I wanted to stay at my foster family. My foster brother was 19 and he was nice to me, I went to school, I had enough to eat, it was a good place, and when the foster family weren't angry with me, they were good to me.

But there were bad things there as well. The parents didn't help me to do my homework, they wanted me to help in the house and garden; cleaning, growing vegetables, walking the dogs, chopping and carrying wood. When I misbehaved, they would beat me with a slipper or with the sole of a rubber boot on my bottom. They punished me this way often. Now, when I think back, I realise that sometimes I was wrong, that I made mistakes, but sometimes it wasn't for my fault that they beat me. Sometimes I think I would like to be back, but other times I am glad I'm not, because it is good here.

I lived in that family for five years. At first, my older brother was with me, but he was moved to a different foster family, and then he went to technical college. I don't know what family he was moved to, so I don't know what college he goes to and I can't contact him. The last thing that I remember that went wrong there was one day I was doing my homework and I couldn't understand it, so I asked for help and they didn't help. They said I had to do it by myself, so then there was an argument, angry words, and I said I didn't want to live with them any more. They said, fine, we will do the paperwork and you can live somewhere else! And that was that. Then I came here.

**Kolya's Story
The To Russia
With Love
View**

"He is easy to work with and psychologically stable."

Kolya is a good boy and a quiet boy. His interests are more for a younger age group than his own – he didn't have a childhood, not a real one, so he is very immature. He still likes playing with teddy bears and will curl up in the play-tent and cuddle them. But he is keen to share what he learns with the other children, is easy to work with and psychologically stable. He's a good student, but needs direction. He can achieve, but needs help to do so because his tendency is to choose the easy option and not stretch himself.

His Irish holiday had a huge impact on him, he feels loved now. He feels better about himself since he came back. He feels worth something now.

Before the foster family I lived in an orphanage in Bryansk, but that was a bad place. I had my brother with me, so I was left alone. I am sorry that I am not in touch with him any more. He was good at protecting me. Debbie is going to try to find him.

In the very beginning I lived with my biological family, but I don't remember much about that. My mum was deprived of parental rights, no one knew where my father was. Now they are both dead. The only thing I remember about my mum is she had blonde hair. I don't know why she was deprived of her rights.

When I lived with her, I remember I had a bike, I watched cartoons on TV, sometimes we went for a walk. One day when I was six I was told by my foster family that my parents were dead.

I don't know how either of them died and I didn't go to their funerals because I only found out afterwards. I went to the grave-yard once, where they are buried. I have no photos of my parents.

I don't know if I have grandparents or any other family. I miss my parents, because I don't have them, so that makes me sad. Sometimes I miss my foster family, but mostly I miss my biological parents, even though I don't remember them. They were my family.

I would love another family, I would go straight away, I wouldn't even think about it. As long as they look kind and not cross. It's better in a family than in an orphanage because you have more places you can go and things you can do. Here, even though the carers are kind to us, we are always in one place, I like when Mairtin teaches me the guitar. In a family, you can play outside for longer, here there is so much routine, always some task we need to do.

I went to Ireland this year for two weeks and met a beautiful family there, I wish they were my family."

Sasha (12).

Sasha has lived in Hortolova for four years. He is a silent, awkward child and found it difficult to answer questions or talk much about his past

----

"The best thing about living here is that there are people here who will help us. The worst thing is when people fight. The boys fight more than the girls, and I fight too, often, but I don't like it, it just happens to me.

I have lived here for four years now. Before that I lived in a small town, five or six hours away, with my foster family – my mum, my brother, my sister and my dad. I don't know where my parents are. I don't know if they are alive. I don't know if I have any brothers or sisters anywhere in the world.

The foster family was a good family, they were kind to me. We went shopping, to the merry-go-round and they bought me ice-cream. There was very seldom fighting when I was with the family. I was there for six years, since I was about two. I knew they were my foster family, not my real family, because they told me.

One day I stopped living with them. My foster father started drinking heavily. He was very violent and started beating my foster mum. There was lots of beatings for my Mama and he was beating me as well. He didn't beat his own children, just my foster mum and me. Then my foster mum died and my foster father was drinking almost every day, for about two years. I was going to school every day but nobody noticed or asked me anything. Then one day a man came and took me, a man from the government. He

**Sasha's Story
The To Russia
With Love
View**

"He loses his temper and his grip on his emotions very easily; anything at all can set him off."

Sasha is a very emotional boy, and he doesn't cope well with his emotions. The distance between being very aggressive and very happy is short for him. He is bright and successful at school, but he does not apply any real effort to what he does. He is careless; if he paid more attention, he would do even better. He is very sporty, he'll play anything and is very energetic. He also likes reading and art. Sasha is always at the centre of everything, with the girls as well as the boys. He has a charismatic personality, but he can be rude too. If the other children are sitting quietly, not paying him attention, he will tease and tease until they pay him attention.

He loses his temper and his grip on his emotions very easily; anything at all can set him off. He is ready to explode at any time. When angry or upset, he is very aggressive, physically and verbally. When we see him getting too wild, we stop whatever it is he's doing, give him a book and tell him to go and read.

That works well for him. He likes one-to-one attention.

didn't tell me why they were taking me away, just that because I am a foster child, my foster father was deprived of his parental rights for me, not for his own children, so they stayed with the father but I was taken.

Even though it was bad, I didn't want to leave, I wanted to stay there. I miss my brother and sister, we don't have any contact. When I grow up, I want to be a policeman. To chase bad guys and help good people."

Nikita (8).

Nikita has lived in Hortolova for two years. His sister is with a foster family, and Nikita believes that the family will take him too. However, staff at Hortolova are much less sure of this.

"I don't remember what my parents looked like, but I remember their names. My mama is called Natasha, my father is Dima. She is in a village far away from here, but I don't know exactly where and I am not in touch with her. It was good when I lived with her, but my mum didn't care for us very well. My sister made food for us, not my mum.

She didn't get angry with us, she just didn't take care of us. One day when I was five people came to look at the house and they took me and my sister to the shelter house because my mum was drinking and smoking.

From the shelter house we went to a foster family for one years, but they didn't finish the paperwork to keep us and so we went back to the shelter house. There was never any trouble, nothing bad happened, they just didn't do the paperwork. With my foster family it was good, there was my foster mum and dad and two brothers. I helped my mum to feed the chickens. We lived in a village, and I helped her and played with her. I was sorry to leave.

I have lived here for two years. It's ok. I wasn't afraid when I came here. I like football and PE. When I grow up, I want to be a footballer and play for Barcelona. I train a lot, I practise. The carers want to take me to a football club outside Hortolova, to train more. My sister now lives with a second foster family, I see her in the holidays when they

Nikita's Story
The To Russia
With Love
View

"He believes that in September he will go to the foster family where his sister is already living."

On first impressions, Nikita can seem quiet and sweet. He is a nice-looking boy and can seem very appealing. But he is very aggressive when upset, and he is very quick to get upset. His moods are very changeable. He fights with the other boys and with the carers. If someone bumps into him, or says something in the wrong tone of voice, he can get upset and angry, but he gets out of it quickly as well and doesn't sulk. Nikita is very sporty, he always asks for jerseys, football boots and sports gear for presents. He is cheeky, he likes prizes and rewards; everything he does, he wants to be rewarded for it. If you sit beside him when he is doing work or art, he does ok, but left to himself, he doesn't finish, he doesn't make an effort or try. He believes that in September he will go to the foster family where his sister is already living, but no one is certain if this is going to happen yet. He has set his heart on it, but we don't know for sure if they will take him, or if they only visit for the sake of his sister.

Also, Nikita is a very difficult boy, and not every family would be willing to take him on.

Whenever a foster family comes, the children behave like little angels, they want so badly to be fostered that they wont put a foot wrong or do anything to show what they can be like.

take me as well. When I stay with them, they are very kind, they say they will take me next September and I will live with them. They took my sister first, then started to visit me because she wanted to see me. They have already started the paper work, and in September I will go and live with them."

"What shines through is their lack of sophistication – they have never heard of Man Utd, Chelsea, Disneyland."

Roma (12).

One of the few boys who seems his age. Roma has a nice deep voice, a confident open face, and direct and friendly manner.

"I have lived here for two years, and I like it very much. I have friends, I have good carers, I like studying, and just to be here. I like PE, computers, and maths. Its not hard for me to learn about these things, I am clever.

Before Hortolova, I lived about 30mins walk from here, in a little village. I lived in a foster family – mama, papa and me – for two years. It was a very isolated house, just a cottage with four fields and a pond, no neighbours, no other children to play with. But I had friends from another town who I knew from school, and they would visit me on their bikes.

It was good living there. My foster parents didn't drink, except when they celebrated something, and then only a little bit. They were farmers, but I don't think it is such an interesting job, I would not like to do that when I grow up.

Sometimes I misbehaved and my parents were cross with me. When that happened, they hit me. Sometimes they used the belt, when I was really bad, but if I was not too bad, they just asked me not to do that again. I didn't help them to clean the house, I was untidy and sometimes I went wild and misbehaved. I cut a curtain. I didn't mean to; I was playing with a knife and I tried it out on the curtain and it got cut. But they were very angry. They said I started a fire and so they didn't want to keep me, but I didn't do it. I would prefer to live still with them, I see them sometimes still; I went

**Roma's Story
The To Russia
With Love
View**

"He is very affectionate and trustworthy and has very little aggression."

Roma is a very good child, he is more like a family child than an orphan, because he is not institutionalised. He is very bright, successful in school and reliable. If you ask him to do something, you can trust that he will do it meticulously. He has many talents and can dance and sing as well as play sport and study. He is very affectionate and trustworthy and has very little aggression; he might answer back, but he doesn't have tantrums or anger issues.

He likes talking to different people, he can discuss his situation confidently, without getting upset. He doesn't swear and has never said a bad word about his foster parents, even though they rejected him. They live about 20mins walk from here, but they don't visit him.

We still can't understand what happened there. He says there was no conflict, no fights. But it seems as though something happened to make them reject him. It is possible he just doesn't want to talk about it.

But it is also possible that the foster parents have their own issues and simply didn't want to keep him. Sometimes, if the foster parents just don't want to keep a child, they will say the child has problems and behavioural issues, and it may not be true.

Roma says he wants to go to the vocational school and train to be a chef, but he is very bright and we will encourage him to aim for something higher. Among his age-group in Hortolovoa, Roma is the most likely to succeed materially in life.

He needs extra grinds and a more challenging curriculum, but we will ensure he gets these, and the support he needs to meet the challenge.

back to visit them once since I came to live here. My biological parents separated when I was young. They live somewhere in the Bryansk region, but I don't know where, I don't see them. They were drunk all the time and it was not much fun living with them.

I have two sisters and three brothers, but they are grown up and independent. I am the youngest, so it was just me at home with my mother and father. Normally I played with my friend outside, to keep out of the house. If I needed food, I got it for myself, and I didn't go to school very often. Sometimes my parents had arguments and fights because they were drunk. My mum was good, but dad beat me sometimes.

My mum brought me to the shelter house because we didn't have any money, so she gave me to the people in the shelter house to care for me. She visited me only once, and after that I didn't see her again. I don't know where my brothers and sisters are, and they don't know where I am so I don't know how we will ever be in touch.

I stayed in the shelter house until I was 9. It was ok there, I had friends. Then I went to the foster family, and then they didn't want me anymore. They brought me to hospital where I stayed for a few days, then back to the shelter home, and then here. I don't know why they didn't keep me. I don't remember what the last bad thing I did was, I think there wasn't anything much. They just got sick and tired that I didn't help them around the house. I would have liked them to keep me, but I suppose they got sick of me.

When I leave here, I would like to be a chef. I can cook omelette and soup. It would be an interesting job, you can cook tasty things for yourself. No one ever asked me so many questions before, but I don't mind."

Kyrill (11).

Kyrill has been living in Hortolova for nearly a year. Small and thin, he seems much younger than he is. He speaks in a high, piping voice and doesn't make eye-contact.

"I like it here, its beautiful. I like football, basketball, and most of all I like reading – especially fairytales. I like the performances and concerts that we have and the food is good.

Before I came here, I lived with my granny, but she died because of my dad, and mum left us, she went to a village and she died as well, about three years ago. I don't know why my mother went away, she went to visit someone and she didn't come back. I was very upset, we didn't even talk so I couldn't ask her to come back. She didn't say goodbye or tell me she was going.

Mum had many guests all the time when she lived with us, relatives who would come for celebrations. She was a good cook, my favourite food was the dumplings she made, and she did my homework with me. Dad wasn't angry when my mum was living with us.

We had a house made of white bricks and a fence and a garden behind the house. We had a TV and couches and the house was in a town but I don't remember the name of the town. We had a dog and many cats. I miss having animals here; we have one dog, but he is for everyone, not just me. I had books at home, I always was reading. When I think back, the things I miss most are my dog, and a cat, and TV.

Dad didn't work, he just stayed in the house, drinking and smoking. He was always shouting and screaming at me and he beat

**Kyrill's Story
The To Russia
With Love
View**

"We try and deal with this now, becaus[e]
aggression, so we try and deal with thi[s]

We don't know much about Kyrill's family, except that his granny was raising him and then she died, and that's how he came here. He has some difficulties with his speech and some intellectual problems. It seems as if no one paid much attention to his education before now, and he had to repeat the first year in school when he came here.

He had an operation at some stage, he has a scar on his chest, but no one knows exactly what it was from and he doesn't remember. We presume it was for a heart operation, and so he is on a heart specialist list and we bring him regularly for check-ups and try to monitor him.

Kyrill doesn't talk much about what happened to him, but psychological or physical abuse would be typical in these families, which in his case is probably where his intellectual and speech difficulties started.

We know he didn't have many friends in his other school, and that the other children teased him.

Here, the children try and tease him too, but we keep an eye on that and prevent it.

He can get very defensive and aggressive, and he is very tense. We try and deal with this now, because the older a boy gets, the more surely this turns into aggression, so we try and deal with this it now, and teach him how to handle his feelings. He

my granny and I don't like seeing that. But he was not angry every day. Sometimes he didn't drink, sometimes he did. When my granny ran out of her pension money, he didn't drink because he the older a boy gets, the more surely this turns into it now, and teach him how to handle his feelings."

frequently pushes and shoves the other children and can be very diffi-cult. He is like a match, he goes up in flames of anger so fast. Kyrill doesn't participate much in school, he knows he is slower than other children and for a long time wouldn't put his hand up.

He has very poor attention span and can't concentrate even on a very short story.

This is because of his develop-mental delay. But we have seen positive changes since he is with us.

His memory has improved signifi-cantly, at first he couldn't remember even two or three words, now he can learn poems.

A multi-functional team including the psychologist, teachers and carers, try to support and help him. He is just about coping with the school curriculum for the moment, if he stops coping then it will be a different story and he might be moved to another orphanage, but we hope that will not happen.

He has a sister who has been fostered with distant relatives who calls me regularly, so I get Kyrill and we talk to her. She really loves him and cares for him. He is lucky.

It is hard to say what will happen with him, but we haven't yet found any talents or interests that we can work on, to try and develop and shape a future career, but we hope we will."

couldn't buy it. And then he was kind.

Dad didn't beat my sisters, just me. He didn't beat me much, only sometimes and not too badly, but he was quite severe with my granny, a few times he beat her with a chair. I tried to protect granny, but dad was too drunk and I was too small. When I saw him getting angry, I would try to talk to him, but he would never listen. I feel angry with him because he wasn't good to my granny. I will be different when I am a father. I will work, and I will look after my children.

I have two sisters, both older than me. Aliona was taken by a foster family, and my other granny took my other sister, Irina. My sisters love me.

When I left my home, my sister said we had to go to the hospital. I wanted to run away from there, to go home, but then a lady came after a while, and she took Aliona to a family and she brought me here.

"Mum was a good cook, my favourite food was the dumplings she made, and she did my homework with me. Dad wasn't angry when my mum was living with us."

I didn't know where I was going when they took me away. I was afraid because I didn't know what to expect. But I was happy when I saw the place. It's better here, because dad was always angry and drunk. This is a more calm place to live, that is a good thing. No one is shouting. I like to be around many children, and here there are lots of people to play with.

My sister Irina and my granny visit me when I have holidays in school, at Christmas and summer. We go for a walk in the woods. I would love to see my dad, but he never visits me. I like when Moscow visitors come and bring us good things. They are Debbie's friends. Christmas here is good because of the Moscow people.

"Their touching faith, the childish attempts they have made to hold their families together, the hope they still have that someone will one day come for them."

"Now, my only focus is to ensure the charity survives, because we are just about holding our heads above water."

What the future holds
Debbie Deegan

So what next for To Russia With Love? Where do we go from here? Debbie Deegan on what the future holds for her, her team, and the programme.

Frankly, my only goal at the moment is survival. There was a time when my goal was more and more wonderful programs, when all I thought about was enhancing the basic love and care that we give our children; getting them to skating classes, music lessons, reunification of siblings, socialisation trips, sporting competitions, meeting with grandparents, finding mothers. Now, my only focus is to ensure the charity survives, because we are just about holding our heads above water.

It is very hard to survive right now. First the Celtic Tiger kicked us all in the stomach – there's no doubt about that. We were bent over and in pain, but we were just about getting through it; people felt sorry for charities because they knew we had been so hard-hit and so they continued to give what little they could. Then along came the CRC and Rehab scandals, and that crushed us. Those scandals gave people a reason to stop giving, and worse, a reason to stop trusting – you could almost see them wondering 'is she on a huge salary? Is this going towards her pension or health insurance?' I have lived all my life in Clontarf, and would always have been a huge supporter of the CRC. I spent summers there washing dishes as a teenager, just like everyone else. The whole community supported and trusted them. But that trust was totally and utterly abused, and we all felt the pain of it.

What has saved us has been our shop, With Love. We set this up a year ago, and it has been almost our sole source of income since January. It's a charity shop, but the cutest, prettiest, best-run charity shop you can think of. We get wonderful clothes and items donated by generous people – we have sold Jimmy Choo shoes, Diane von Furstenburg dresses, David Emanuelle ball-gowns, Louis Vuitton bags – and we have made it look so gorgeous that people are in and out all the time. The window is a showstopper thanks to one of the best window dressers in Ireland, and an old friend, Aideen Linnane.

Women pop in to chat and hang out as much as to buy, but once there, they always find something they want. Everyone is very comfortable being there, because we have gorgeous volunteers working who are warm and welcoming.

It pays our bills – office rent, our light and heat, staff costs, and our programme costs in Russia. Without the shop and our gorgeous customers, in truth, we would be gone.

Even so, we have cut ourselves to the bone, and that is despite the tireless efforts of the amazing people who fundraise for us, some of whom have been doing this for 15 years now, including the Billy Barry Stage School, Rosemary Lennon Maher, John Clancy, Kim McKayed and the management and staff of Supervalu – the list goes on and on.

I used to have seven full-time staff in Dublin, now there is just one full timer, the lovely Jenny, and one full time volunteer, the most caring girl you could ever hope to meet, Grainne O'Driscoll, helped by Dara Ferguson and Jennifer McKeown. In Russia, working directly with the children, there are six of them, all angels.

In Moscow, we are lucky enough to be supported by two beautiful Russian businesswomen, founder of English Nursery School Moscow, Maria Gremitskikh, and her daughter Anna Nikolaeva. They have brought so much to our children.

People text or ring and say 'can you ask your office to send us your audited reports...' These days, I am the office. There is no 'us' – my unpaid accountants, Fergal McGrath, is worn out with me and my endless expectations – as is the unstoppable John Darcy.

Pressure is heavier and heavier trying to keep up with the many auditing and administration requirements of running a charity. It is very hard to keep going, keeping all the balls in the air. I have a great team of women volunteers around me, many of whom are still here 16 years later, who help out in all sorts of ways, but staff? Keeping a skeleton staff is tough going.

So far, we haven't really let the children be affected by the damage to charities in Ireland. We have cut so many programs that inevitably there has been an effect on them, but we try to minimise that, and the basic structure of care around each child is unchanged.

The person most affected by the reduced funds is me, because I still try to cover as much ground. And yes, I understand all about the burn-out theory, but the only solution is to do less, and that I just can't do, not when I know what my doing less means to our children.

The last few years have been personally very difficult. This was never a job for me, always a passion, never a project I felt I could walk away from when the going got rough. Every day we are sponges for our children's tears, pain, heartache.

Because of this, we insist that every volunteer goes through a process of de-briefing once they come back from Russia. If we were all social workers or psychologists, we would have to off-load regularly to a professional. None of us really do this. We do hear way too much, and we do take it all into our own hearts and try and ease their pain.

I insist on this for others, but I never do it myself. I am 16 years in Russia now, and I think because I am a talker that I don't need it. However, if I feel it is all too much after a trip, then I do have some support systems in place. Dr Peter Hanlon is my 'unpaid' therapist, and one who 'gets me' – too well actually. He allows me vomit out words and makes me look at the madness of the world I work in. I argue with him all the time though. And I don't listen to his advice, even though I know it is right. He is one of my scaffoldings.

My dear friends that I treasure in Russia and Ireland are another. I am surrounded by them, and I am so lucky with them. Some are lifelong friends, some not, but all are very special people. My beautiful children, who are endlessly patient, and have no trouble with sharing me out to so many.

Sophie in particular, has been my fellow traveller, advisor, typist, event manager, organiser, you name it, for years, she is endlessly calm except when my e-mails start beeping into her phone from 5.00am. It just drives her nuts. She now has a real job, with a real salary, and I miss her every day. I don't think she misses me though!

She has been an incredible support, as beautiful on the inside as she is on the outside. She will never really escape it. Like me, she loves Russia, so it is discussed every day, usually at 7.00am when I am full of great ideas. For some reason this also drives her mad. And I send the dogs in to wake her, so I don't get blamed for that bit.

My wonderful husband, who stands beside me every step of the way. I have no idea how he is still there. My lifelong best friend, who knows every detail of my life, who listens, and never judges. My Mammy, the best Mammy there is, she makes all our lives easier, and better. My board, who mind me, trust me, advise me and are strong guardians to the children. These people are all scaffolding.

And Connemara. Beautiful Connemara, that has been a refuge to many of our children over the years, and ultimately a place of calm for me. I am welcomed there like one of their own. I love the air, the mystical rainbows, the ocean, Sky Road, Mannin Bay, my turf fires, the silence. It is one of the most beautiful places on earth, and is definitely therapy for my head. I could not have managed without it over the years. All this is the scaffolding that has kept me sane after too many years of endless broken hearts.

We have an office in Moscow now, with two staff, and Russia is slowly staring to yield funds. However, it is very slow – far slower even than we thought – and the process is very top-heavy and bureaucratic. Those beginning to give money are international companies with established Corporate Social Responsibility (CSR) policies who are based in Moscow, rather than Russian companies, who are still very slow to give to charity. The multi-nationals are very cautious, and they are right to be, because there are so many ways the money can be misused or misappropriated, but we are a really good fit because we are absolutely transparent and lily-white, and so they are starting, gradually, to listen to us.

Even among Russia companies, it is becoming a bit trendy, now, to help orphanages. Sixteen years ago when I started, it wasn't trendy at all. Frankly, it was like working with rats. All I heard was honest bafflement – 'why do you want to help these children?' But the psyche is gradually, grindingly, changing. The current political situation is, sadly, another huge challenge for us to cope with, as Corporate Social Responsibility is not high on people's agendas right now.

This small Moscow fundraising office is a viable, self-sustaining future for To Russia With Love. Ultimately, we hope to wind Dublin down and concentrate our efforts in Moscow, but for now we are still hugely dependent on the generosity of Irish people to keep us going. Moscow is much slower to take off than we thought it would be. I have great connections in Russia, lots of celebrity friends who have the affection and respect of millions of Russian people, but in my experience, celebrities don't give you money. They will give you their time, their presence in a photo, their endorsement, but not actual money. And so even with these connections, it is a long, hard slog.

As for the children, yes, we should by now be looking at fostering, at big broad programmes to get all children out of orphanages and into family situations. But we are not there yet. It isn't possible. And so, on a day-to-day basis, we are holding their hands when they have period pains or a headache, comforting them when they feel sad and lonely. We're stuck in the forest and we can't get out of it. Not yet.

For now, if we can get our children to normal, we feel we have succeeded. If we can get them to grow up and feel as if they are someone, that is our measure of success. If they are ready to get a job, get married, we know we have triumphed. We are interjecting self-esteem at a very late stage. Psychologists would say it's too late to do it, but we have proved that it isn't.

We get children at 9 or 10, who have no thoughts of self-worth at all, and by the age of 18 they are ready to move on, go to college, live by themselves and take on the world. These were kids who nobody in the world loved; considering we are intervening at such a late stage, we have amazing results. Our intervention works. We have proved it, time and again.

We are building a stronger child, so that by the time they leave, they feel as good as anyone else. That growth comes through a tapestry of different things, all the many things we do with and for our children, everything from a hand to hold to extra lessons.

We need approximately €250,000 a year to sustain all we do, and to continue to change the lives of many. It is not a huge sum, but it is bloody hard to find.

Honestly, we are on our knees. We are doing our best to find funds wherever we can; Russia or Ireland, or anywhere in between. If you know anyone that wants to help us, please call me. I am always available.

As I finish this book, I am in Connemara. I have just sent home two beautiful Russian children, who wept buckets of tears in Departures. They had the best two weeks of their lives, surrounded by love in an incredible family in Galway. We do not normally bring children here, but these two were a special case. They were a joy to be with, but it is a heart-break to watch how they are so unused to the simple things. I blow dried Sasha's hair, she was enraptured at the touch.

I snuggled under a blanket with Kolya and we watched a Zombie movie, he squealed his way though it, making me eat his jellies with him. He was in heaven with the attention. Small things, but so valuable to them.

There is a team of incredible women planning a big event this summer for more than 300 people in Clifden, driven by Sharon Griffin of Ohh! By Gum, an adorable shop, with Trina Sweeney and Michele Hehir.

Fourteen single fabulous males are lining up for the first Connemara Man competition; all gorgeous, warm, men. They met our children from Russia last week in Clifden and all fell in love. Thank God this happens, as we badly need people to help us.

I am so impressed that a small town would take this on, would treat me as one of their own, and roll out the red carpet for our children. I am so proud to be Irish. They are the best race in the world for kindness. For 16 years, Irish people have trusted me to take their money to Russia, something that is hard to fathom. Incredible trust, incredible people. I am so grateful.

We cannot do a thing without people's donations: small, medium, large, corporate or personal. We are barely getting through, and we still have armloads of children to stick by. Eventually we won't have – they will be in families or small residential units, where they should be – but until that day comes, please trust us with your €5, your €50, or more if possible. If you want to make a difference in the life of an abandoned child, use us as your conduit to do that. We need you badly. If you have been moved by the children's stories, please take the time to full in one of the one-off gift donation or direct debit forms we have attached to the book.

I do not know what the children would do without us and everyone who is behind us.

Please, if you do give this year, think of the stories you have just read, and help us get these children through the next few years.

I am happy to stay by their side. *Please stay by mine.*

✳

Epilogue
Egor Zubets

A preface to a Russian edition that will never be.

I have no right to be even the smallest part of this book. I have no history with To Russia With Love, I'm an ordinary Muscovite from a happy family with two sisters, a dozen cousins and three children of my own. We care about each other, love and protect each other. My children are quite normal family children, with Saturday dinners at my grandmother's place and holidays in a big crowd of relatives. Way too far from orphanages, from abuse, lack of love and emotions.

However I know Debbie, her family, her colleagues and some of the children you have listened to. I bumped into Debbie's life a few years ago. Unexpectedly, with no obvious reason but with some purpose for sure. I went to Bryansk, met the children and was left absolutely motivated – but this is another story. It will take another 16 years of work, maybe, to allow myself to be part of this story.

This book was written for the people from the West. They care, they help and they understand already. Being Russian, I want to talk to Russians. I have always been very proud to be Russian. I still am. But there is something I cannot understand. We talk about our hospitality, our open hearts, our inwardness. We honestly think that we are a better nation than any other. Facing all these sanctions from the West at the moment, we really feel that we are unique.

But when it comes to implementing our uniqueness into real deeds, very few of us can be proud of ourselves. We are willing to help Ukrainians and give them shelter and food for free, we give money to flooded regions to rebuild their houses when asked through TV, we are ready to support many other 'calling' activities.

What I mean is we are ready to fight great battles but prefer not to notice everyday difficulties. To my greatest regret it was a person from the West that showed me the life of the orphans in my country and I'm ashamed of myself, my family and my nation.

If you bought this book as literature, as horror fiction or to confirm what you feel you already know, don't bother reading it. Because even if you know this stuff, you won't care. The only way to read this book is to listen to the children, to feel the kind of empathy that motivates and requires reaction, to help.

I feel that my words will be wasted. Debbie's story was on the main Russian TV channel in Andrey Malakhov's hugely watched chat show. One would have thought that such exposure on a programme watched by so many would have elicited a massive response. On the contrary – the response was pitiful – an indictment of our apathy and inability for action.

"We are not able to change the system" that's what we think, and we carry on undisturbed...

I just don't want this book to face the same ending. I want to be proud of my nation and of myself, no matter how pathetic it may sound. I want to see the changes in our society, I want us Russians to be caring and loving again and I want to be part of it. I'm not against great battles, I just need us to think a bit and to remember that Russians were once ready to stand up for their own people.

TO RUSSIA WITH L♥VE

Text **HUG** to **50300** to donate €4 to our Charity.

100% of text cost goes to To Russia With Love across most network providers.
Some providers apply VAT which means a minimum of €3.26 will go to To Russia With Love.
Service Provider LIKECHARITY 014433890

We need your help.
If you have been moved by the children's stories, please take the
time to full in one of the one-off gift donation or
direct debit forms attached to the book or
please text a €4 donation to the above number.

Thank you.